Mom,

May your
life be full, happy
and healthy and
your feng shui be
perfect always.

I love you,

Esha

SLEUTH YOUR HOUSE — HEAL YOUR LIFE

Adventures of a Feng Shui Detective

SLEUTH YOUR HOUSE — HEAL YOUR LIFE

Adventures of a Feng Shui Detective

VALMAI HOWE ELKINS

Woodley & Watts
MONTREAL · SEDONA · TAOS

Woodley & Watts
400 McGill, 3rd Floor
Montreal, QC
Canada
H2Y 2G1

Canadian Cataloguing in Publication Data
Howe Elkins, Valmai
Sleuth Your House, Heal Your Life: Adventures of a Feng Shui Detective

ISBN 0-9698972-6-X

ACKNOWLEDGMENTS
The author wishes to express warmest gratitude to Sylvie Arvanitakis, Denise Bernier, Beth Katz, Elaine Mackasey, Elliott Mitchell and Madeleine Partous for their generous help with the manuscript, to Patricia Chang for her support and enthusiasm, and to Tilke Elkins and David Elkins for their constant faith, humor, love and wisdom.

Author's photograph, back flap, by Tom Rush
Cover design by Tilke Elkins
Inside design, layout and production by Sylvie Arvanitakis

*For David, Tilke, Jonathan, Heather, Madeleine and Parker John
and in loving memory of Theodore "Teddy" Wu*

Contents

Contents

Contents

Contents

The Journey

*T*he practice of Feng Shui helps improve your life by creating harmony in your home. The idea is that the floor plan, the placement of your furniture and the colors you use can increase or decrease your happiness.

But before you move a single piece of furniture, let's take a look at what's already there. In this book we'll be examining what your house is really saying about you. First let me explain how I began my fascinating examination of the outer clues which reveal our inner story.

I have, since childhood, been fascinated by the rooms I've lived in; the colors, textures, placement of furniture and objects. But until I was introduced to the formal principles of Feng Shui, I was unable to consciously apply these childhood insights. Indeed, throughout childhood it seemed as though I were pulled in two different directions. While I had a firm belief in "magic," the idea that if you believed in something it would happen, that anything was possible, at the same time I felt helpless, particularly to understand my emotions and relationships.

For seventeen years I worked with women and men in childbirth; the miracle of birth was as magical as I could wish for, and gave me enormous joy. Perhaps it resonated with my profound need to give birth to my own potential.

The last thing I wanted was to explore childhood pain. I was so happy to be free from the old constrictions. At least I thought I was free.

I had enormous energy and enthusiasm and it was easy for me to plunge wholeheartedly into preparing parents for birth, writing birthing books, traveling, lecturing and helping set up hospital birthing rooms. The work I did was valuable and gave me great satisfaction. But I was not living harmoniously. The phone rang constantly. Even the times when I was breastfeeding my daughter were interrupted by the jangle. I discovered the telephone answering machine the first year they came out, but the scores of calls required a response. I was juggling marriage, motherhood and a career.

The publication of my first book, *The Rights of the Pregnant Parent* with Canadian, U.S., Australian and French editions thrust me into the public eye with a magnitude I'd never imagined. I was twenty five years old.

I loved the speaking trips to Australia, Britain and throughout the U.S. and Canada, sharing my ideas with wonderful people, but the pace was hectic. Once, in seventeen days, I counted thirty five radio and television appearances, seven major public lectures of anywhere from five hundred to two thousand people and an endless succession of press interviews, airports and hotel rooms.

I was grateful for the dramatic response to the book, but it was not good for my family life. I recall one evening, standing by the phone in our kitchen, while my husband, David, and daughter, Tilke, waited for me at the dining room table with a delicious pizza they'd prepared from scratch. It was one of my childbirth education clients. Her waters had broken and she was having strong contractions. Could I be with her? Still standing, I bolted down my dinner and headed out into the night, leaving David and Tilke disappointed.

Looking back, it was clear that my priorities had become distorted, but at the time I simply kept rushing along with no time for any introspection. Perhaps, had the success come later I might have been able to keep perspective, but in my twenties I had about as much self understanding as a piece of wet toast.

Something was bound to give. My heart attack was a pivotal point. Eventually forced to cut back my teaching and traveling, I reconnected with a childhood dream to write novels. I didn't plan them, I simply sat down at my typewriter and began to write. The material that surfaced was the reservoir of childhood pain. My novels were an exploration and a catharsis which unblocked the door to my quest for self understanding.

Eventually my illness, made worse by bouts of bronchitis and pneumonia, caused my doctor to suggest strongly that I spend the winters in a dry climate.

Through a series of happy circumstances, I found myself a small adobe house in Taos, New Mexico, that mecca for writers and artists made famous by Georgia O'Keeffe and D.H. Lawrence. It was there, in the shadow of a mountain considered sacred by the Tewa indians, that I was introduced to Feng Shui.

The moment I began to apply the principles to my own life it was as though I'd been given a key. Suddenly I was aware of what I'd been creating all my life. I could now begin to unblock old restrictions and create harmony.

Later, when I became a practitioner, I applied these principles to help others. It was clear that our dwellings affect us. I learned the traditional "corrections" and "cures."

Then shortly after I became a practitioner I had a revelation. Not only do our dwellings AFFECT us, they also REFLECT us.

I discovered an unexpected gift. Without knowing anything about my client ahead of time, working only with environmental "clues" I was able to describe in precise detail what had occurred in that person's life and how it was currently affecting her or him.

So precise was the information I could often pinpoint such things as the age at which childhood traumas occurred, and whether the block was created with the mother, father, both parents or some other circumstance.

Once the old blocks were identified, the way to remove them was clearly revealed.

The results were miraculous. I watched in awe as my clients transformed their lives and went on to create harmony and "fortunate blessings."

This ability to help people create harmony in their lives through the use of Feng Shui, continues unabated. The telephone still jangles but my reaction today is quite different. I just had a call, for example, from Carmen, a client I'd worked with several months ago. After my assessment she confirmed the findings: she was feeling stuck in her current job, to the point where depression had set in. Though she had once been a promising artist, she hadn't painted for a long time, indeed her work was stacked in the garage facing the wall. Throughout her house were clues which indicated difficulty with her parents and a lack of self confidence in her ability to support herself doing what she loved to do. After completing the suggested changes, she described an initial feeling of clarity. This afternoon she was bubbling.

"I just wanted to tell you about all the great new work offers I've been getting. I'm having more fun than I've had in a long time. As part of my Feng Shui plan I'd hung a pair of dolphins, you'd mentioned to choose a symbol of a happy family. I chose the dolphins because somehow for me they represented a happy family. You won't believe this. I've been invited to take part in a singing workshop in Florida. I love singing. And we get to swim with dolphins!" She rushed on, "And I met with my father last week in Los Angeles. It was the nicest time we've ever had together. There was a financial issue that's been a problem between us for about a year. Well, we got it resolved without dragging up any of the old stuff... that all seems to be gone and there's just this feeling of clarity!"

Each day I'm privileged to share my clients' stories that, like Carmen's, commence with a new feeling of clearness.

Where does the process begin and how does it work? Though Carmen's changes may sound magical, and indeed they are, they are not mysterious. Each improvement in her life was the result of careful, methodical changes she made in her house. Not that they happened overnight. Feng Shui is not a quick fix. It's a process of consciously unblocking our limitations and creating a solid foundation which will serve us the rest of our lives.

Let's examine the basic assumptions of Feng Shui. If, like the Taoist monks who first revealed the secrets of Feng Shui, we recognize that everything is connected by constantly changing energy then it is easy to understand how we create in the objects around us, reflections of our inner blueprint of energy.

When I wrote my two novels, people asked repeatedly, "Are your books autobiographical?"

I believe that every writer's work is autobiographical, from Colette to Hemingway. I don't mean that the novel is an account of the writer's life, a documentary. I mean that from our inner world, we create characters and themes that reflect our particular view of the outer world. Thus, while my first novel, *The Dreams of Zoo Animals,* appears to parallel my own coming of age in Australia, it is more a re-creation of my feelings of constriction and helplessness than an autobiography.

My consultations with hundreds of clients have confirmed that though our choice of dwelling affects us, our choice is an exquisite reflection of our inner life. Why, for example, are we drawn to a particular piece of artwork? Taste? Yes, but taste is, I believe, simply a resonance with our past experience of who we are.

Examining my own experience, I see that in order for me to become a Feng Shui practitioner, it was essential to begin with my own past, to see what I had created.

I began by asking the question, What sort of little girl was I?

The early days

"What do you want to be when you grow up?" my parents' friends asked. I think if I'd said, "I want to do Feng Shui," I'd have been sent to my room for being cheeky. Fortunately, I'd never heard the words. What I wanted to be was a magician and a detective... and a writer... and make wonderful places to live in... and along the way make myself and other people happy. But I was a child my somewhat tactless aunt referred to as "bashful." I detested that word. I blushed whenever an adult asked personal questions. So I'd mumble, "I never want to grow up." That seemed to amuse them. They'd smile and turn away to resume their conversations while I took the opportunity to disappear.

Of course I knew what I wanted to be. The same as I was then. I was a detective and I was a writer. I was passionate about designing and decorating my cubby houses and I enjoyed taking care of my animals who, when they answered at all, said exactly what I expected them to.

My relationships with people left me feeling helpless. When I asked my mother why grown-ups seemed so unhappy, she replied, "You'll understand when you grow up." I vowed I'd never let that happen.

At bedtime, my mother opened the window to strengthen my health, described by silver-haired Dr. Kilmier as "delicate." Then she fastened the blue wooden shutters against the big hungry Australian mosquitoes.

After she kissed me and said goodnight, I'd lie in bed and count slowly to one hundred. Not a sound from the hallway. Only the swish of the sprinkler on the roses. From then on it was routine: stuff a rolled up blanket in the bed, pull my older brother's pants and sweater over my pajamas, collect my flashlight, notebook and pencil, climb onto the windowsill, unlock the shutters and lower myself into the damp rose-garden, doing my best to avoid the thorns.

The making of a detective

I'd trained myself to move like a shadow, pressed to the tall hedges that lined the streets. Notebook in hand, I was ready to catch the wicked people who came out at night. On the surface everything appeared normal, but you never knew when a crime was about to be committed. Who knew when the man arguing with his wife on the verandah might decide to chop off her head? I'd read about that sort of thing on the front page of TRUTH, the tabloid displayed on the wire rack at Mr. Thorpe's, the newsagent's store.

That ordinary black Studebaker might be a getaway car; jot down the plate number. No, train yourself to remember it in case you're captured. Ha, here comes a couple, it's late, they're up to no good, the man's carrying a little boy fast asleep. A sleeping potion. Probably going to sell him. They're getting in the car, good, you've got the license number. Now, what's that man doing walking alone so slowly. No dog.

When I was about nine I began to hang out in the criminology section of the public library after school. Many years later, on my first trip to Washington D.C., I'd spend most of my visit in the Forensic Department of the FBI.

My favorite game was Kim's Game from Rudyard Kipling's book. *Kim* was my idol, a reckless Delhi street urchin recruited by British Intelligence who trained him systematically to remember complex details. Items were placed on a copper tray. After a brief glance at them, the tray was covered with a paper. At first, Kim was pleased that he could recall the number and colors of jewels on the tray, until a young Indian apprentice outdid him with astonishing details:

"First, are two flawed sapphires — one of two ruttees and one of four as I should judge. The four ruttee sapphire is chipped at the edge. There is one Turkestan turquoise, plain with black veins, and there are two inscribed — one with a name of God in gilt, and the other being cracked across, for it came out of an old ring, I cannot read. We have now all five blue stones. Four flawed emeralds there are, but one is drilled in two places, and one is a little carven. There is one piece of old greenish pipe amber, and a cut topaz from Europe. There is one ruby of Burma, of two ruttees, without a flaw, and there is a balas-ruby, flawed, of two ruttees. There is a carved ivory from China representing a rat sucking an egg; and there is last — ah ha! — a ball of crystal as big as a bean set on a gold leaf." Unable to find a handful of rubies and sapphires I compromised with my brother's marble set and some of my father's antique coins.

My early "detective" work gave me two gifts which would serve me well as a Feng Shui practitioner; a photographic memory and the ability to notice apparently unimportant details. I can still bring up on my mental screen the interior of every single house, apartment or office I have Feng Shui'd. The attention to detail alerted me to incongruities — a tell-tale stick or stone in a back yard, a piece of artwork which didn't fit the decor.

By night, my hero, Kim, crept from rooftop to rooftop, peering in windows, listening to forbidden conversations, gathering valuable information that one day could save peoples' lives by preventing an uprising against the British. The sloping slate rooftops of our quiet leafy suburb were too far apart to negotiate, but that didn't affect my fertile imagination. I was Kim of Australia.

After school I'd write up my notes in one of my cubby houses. First came the tree house in the giant pear tree where I could spy on old Mrs. Richard next door without her suspecting anything. I was sure if I watched long enough I'd catch her out; she was so furtive. My vigilance paid off. One hot and sticky afternoon when she was sure nobody was looking, she crouched down behind a lavender bush. Was she going to unearth buried treasure? I adjusted the focus on my mother's opera glasses. But instead of buried treasure, I zoomed in on peach-colored silk bloomers, then Mrs. Richard's generous white buttocks as she peed beside her lemon tree.

I was curiously sensitive to my surroundings, changing the position of furniture, arranging fresh flowers, thinking carefully of color and fabric. Perhaps it was because instead of playing with other children, I'd spent weeks at a time in bed recovering from persistent bouts of bronchitis. Second to Chips, my dog, my friends lived not in the neighborhood but inside the pages of books.

Looking back, I see a small girl with an incongruous British accent that made her the butt of teasing. Painfully shy, she withdrew into a fantasy world, spending hours in the garden beneath an old apple tree, waiting to meet the fairies who never quite managed to appear.

One day, sure that she could fly, she climbed onto the high roof of the stable, spread her arms and jumped, flapping her "wings." As she fell to the ground, a piece of metal protruding from the shed slashed open the inner thigh of her right leg.

I still have the long scar from the sixteen stitches put in by the family doctor. Unfortunately, he was out of surgical thread and had to make do with the ordinary black sewing variety.

After that I gave up my desire to become a magician.

During the weeks I hobbled around on crutches, I discovered *The Book of Oriental Design* which I can still see in splendid glossy detail. My aunt, the one who described me as "bashful," had traveled to China many times, returning with intriguing black lacquered trunks and screens depicting men and women who eyed each other with a lust both formal and tender.

When we visited Aunt Lilian, instead of including me in conversation, she'd suggest I feed her Yorkshire terrier, Tiberius, sweet Arrowroot biscuits. Tiberius was yappy and demanding. I preferred to examine her Chinese objects, fingering the patterns on the shiny black and gold furniture, gazing at the exotic paintings. Then I'd return home and move our furniture.

Mother was baffled by my insistence on rearranging objects in the house. "Why don't you go out and play?"

But I preferred painting the inside of my cubby house or sorting my bookshelf. I think my parents expected me to grow out of this phase, the way my teachers expected me to outgrow the English accent inherited from my grandmother. I didn't.

Physiotherapy

Back then in Australia, women didn't become anything exciting, except if you were very imprudent and got yourself pregnant. There were no female detectives. Most became teachers or nurses. It was understood you'd want to find a husband and raise a family. Writing was considered frivolous, unless you were a man. Women writers were referred to as "lady writers" or "authoresses." And nobody I knew was an interior designer.

Physiotherapy was considered highly suitable for a well-bred young woman. Besides, as the vocational guidance counselor pointed out to my father, it would give me "something to fall back on." What she meant was if nobody wanted to marry me I wouldn't be a financial burden to my family.

From wombs to rooms

My path to becoming a Feng Shui practitioner was circuitous. The job I'd landed in Montreal was Sole Charge Physiotherapist at The Catherine Booth Hospital, a Salvation Army Women's hospital with one of the best prenatal programs in the city.

I was barely twenty years old and had never had a child. To be as close to the birth process as possible, without actually becoming pregnant myself, I moved into the hospital residence, managing to conceal my Siamese kitten, Nicholas, in my room. On hand around the clock, I indulged my fascination with birth and was thrilled to accompany as many women as I could from my classes, through the births of their children. They taught me not only about the physical process, but equally important, about the complex emotional passage of each phase of labor.

For the next seventeen years I worked with women and their families. In a supportive environment, women know how to trust their bodies and give birth. The problem was that the hospital, with its labor beds and sterile delivery rooms interfered with the normal progress.

Take a woman with a normal labor, confine her to bed, hook her up to an intravenous drip and the belts of an electronic fetal heart monitor, examine her internally frequently, speed her labor up with artificial hormones and chances are she'll require an epidural anesthetic, which increases the need for a whole chain of medical "interventions" up to and too often including cesarean delivery. Intervention is a vicious circle. Research indicates that, for the majority of women, the safest, easiest birth occurs when, instead of being confined to bed, the woman can walk around and change position.

The hospital birthing room

The birthing system in North America was changing, a wave that built from the action of a few parents who were prepared to ask for what they wanted and expected to get it.

After a trip to Amsterdam in 1974, I was convinced that we somehow needed to change the philosophy of birthing. In Holland birth is viewed as a normal process rather than something hazardous. True, there will always be a small percentage of women and their unborn babies for whom birth is potentially dangerous; the latest developments in high-risk care are completely justified in these situations.

The skill, I believe, in obstetrics, is to screen pregnancies carefully, giving those women at risk the best in high-risk care, and using the art and science of midwifery for the majority of women. This is the secret of Holland's safe birthing system.

But how to change a philosophy? You can't suddenly walk into a labor-and-delivery suite and announce, birth is normal, out with the equipment. To begin with, you need women and their partners who are educated about the process of birth and prepared to cope with pain by non-medical means such as position, walking, relaxation and emotional support. And you need a staff also prepared to help parents cope in this way.

After much consideration, it seemed to me that the most effective way to change the philosophy was with a physical environment such as the Dutch one-room system or the "Lamaze" room that had been set up in a Massachusetts hospital.

I approached each of the Montreal hospitals. The answer was no. But once an intention is strong, it creates an energy which builds.

Finally, after a meeting, Morrie Gelfand, Chief Obstetrician of Montreal's Jewish General Hospital, invited me to set up a Birthing Room. The hospital had a suitable area that could be adapted, just outside the regular labor rooms. It was 1978 and this would be the first Birthing Room in Canada. I was tremendously excited. Starting with two connected rooms at the end of the row of conventional labor rooms, the best use of the area was clearly a bedroom and a sitting room where relatives and friends could visit and offer support. A room which resembled home as much as possible, would reduce fear and the resulting tension that we know increases pain.

The groundwork for the change in philosophy was preparation of both parents and staff. As this gained momentum, on a sunny summer morning, my husband and I made a trip to Pascal's Furniture Warehouse. We chose a big brass double bed that invited the father to snuggle with his wife in labor, one big enough for both parents to relax during the first breastfeeding after birth. Then we chose a chocolate brown sofa-bed and a rocking chair for the sitting room. We added a wooden coffee table, several lamps, a braided rug, soft brown and yellow flowered wallpaper, deep golden yellow curtains and a fluffy floral comforter.

Looking back from my perspective as a Feng Shui practitioner, the conventional labor rooms with their pale greens, whites and metal beds produced an overabundance of the metal element which overpowers the element of wood, associated with health. It's no accident that the instinctive response of virtually every woman viewing the delivery room for the first time is tension, produced, in large part by the lack of privacy, those pale walls and gleaming metal. And we know now that whatever creates fear and tension also interrupts the normal progress of labor.

Birthing and Feng Shui

The Birthing Room was rich in the wood element; the plants, floral comforter and wallpaper, coffee table and rocking chair. Wood was strengthened by Water, the deep tones of the sofa, the dark paisley of the braided rug. The Fire of the people strengthened the browns and yellows of the Earth element essential in birthing.

What happened? The room was not just a pretty place. By forbidding the use of high-risk interventions in this room, the philosophy could be developed and protected. Mobility was an essential ingredient. If a woman walks and changes her position according to comfort, labor progresses more rapidly (as much as 36 percent faster) than if she is confined to bed. Interventions which back then were routine, such as intravenous attachments, "just in case," routine electronic fetal monitoring which confines a woman to bed, and routine use of epidural anesthesia have been found to increase the risk of fetal heart distress. Thus, medical staff attending women in the Birthing Room agreed to avoid these procedures. If abnormalities were detected, women could easily be transferred to a regular labor and delivery room.

It was fascinating to watch the effects of environment. The first was privacy. In the regular labor rooms, interns and residents thought nothing of entering without knocking, of not introducing themselves, of treating the woman as a nameless "patient." Frequently, the bed was placed so that she couldn't even see who was coming in. In this new environment, staff spontaneously knocked before entering, introduced themselves, much the way they would if they were visitors in the parents' house. The bed was positioned in the Feng Shui "Command Position," facing the entrance. Something wonderful was happening. As the atmosphere became more home-like, parents and staff began to laugh together and to share personal information.

Not surprisingly, the outcome reflected the changes. The results of a lengthy research project revealed that not only was the room as safe as the conventional labor-delivery room, but the rate of medical interventions such as episiotomy, a surgical cut made to enlarge the vaginal opening, dropped. Equally important was the overall conclusion that women and their partners felt better in the home-like environment.

Common sense? Yes, the kind of common sense valued in Feng Shui. We were witnessing an amazing breakthrough. Everyone was talking Birthing Rooms and over the next five years I was invited to present the concept to hospitals across North America. Today, virtually every hospital in the country has a Birthing Room, indeed my stepson Jonathan and his wife, Heather, welcomed our two grandchildren, Madeleine and Parker John, in a room which grew from my consultations.

My work with Birthing Rooms rekindled my long-term fascination with the way our physical environment affects us. I became increasingly aware of the rooms around me.

Love at first sight: adopting old houses

It was love at first sight. David and I were introduced by our mutual friend Georgiana Beale who had been conniving for months to bring us together. Finally, the perfect occasion presented; the christening of her son Colin, whose birth I had attended. We saw each other across a crowded room. That was it.

David had renovated a charming brick row house; he was as obsessive about place as I was. On our first date we rearranged the furniture in his living room. When we'd finished we sat down and surveyed the results. "What do you think of taking the plaster out?" he asked with a dreamy expression I'd soon quickly recognize. "I think there's brick underneath."

"Wonderful."

Next morning we attacked the white plaster with hammers. Fortunately, it was an old house, the wall needed only a little persuasion to drop its whole facade. So engrossed were we, we ignored the front door bell, until the firemen began to hammer on the door. A passer-by had seen the cloud of plaster dust belching from the window and had called 911. That evening we sipped our drinks in the newly cozy living room and congratulated each other. It was the beginning of a lifetime of magical houses.

We were married the following May 9th in the tiny charming village of Peacham, Vermont. The vicar of the pretty white wooden church, Reverend Blankenship Jr., was thrilled; there hadn't been the wedding of an Elkins in Peacham since 1810. Harvard historian Crane Brinton and his wife generously offered his house, formerly The Jonathan Elkins Tavern, for the reception. Jonathan Elkins had come up from Boston and built the tavern in 1792.

It was a magical wedding for another reason. When I was seventeen, my friend Nicola and I had worked as housemaids at The Chalet Mt. Buffalo, in the Victorian Alps. Though rigidly segregated most of the time, staff were permitted once a month to sit in the back row of the hall and join the guests for a movie evening. I recall every detail of the Hayley Mills movie, *Summer Magic*; the big white clapboard house, the rolling green countryside, the lilac hedge. If someone had told me that I would celebrate my marriage to my soul mate in that very house, even I, with my penchant for magic would have been disbelieving! As Hemingway put it in a *A Movable Feast*, we were very poor and loved each other very much. We drove to Hampton Beach, New Hampshire, for our weekend honeymoon. Monday morning I reported back to The Catherine Booth and David to the magazine he edited.

We completed the rented brick row house we'd been playing with; there were only so many walls you could strip down to the brick. Ever since I'd read Gerald Durrell's book, *My Family and Other Animals*, I'd wanted to live and write on the Greek Island of Corfu. David was working on a book. We sold our few pieces of furniture, I took a leave of absence from the Catherine Booth Hospital, we bought tickets to Rome, and with our worldly possessions in twin blue canvas duffle bags and $2,000, we set off.

Villa Mimosa

The tiny stucco house we rented for $50 a month was an eccentric arrangement of two floors connected by an outdoor staircase. Upstairs was a stone-floored bedroom, outside a primitive bathroom. The living room and narrow kitchen were downstairs.

The first week we were there we sat on the terrace shaded by ancient olive trees, sipped cheap retsina and congratulated ourselves on the marvelous view of azure sea below the house and the wonderful garden surrounding us. We set up our portable Hermes typewriters in the living room.

Then the rains came

It rained and rained and rained. The olives creaked in the winds. Our bedroom floor flooded. The house was unheated save for a large unwieldly gas heater we'd christened "Mother." We lugged Mother downstairs in the morning and upstairs at night, through the driving rain as we slipped on the picturesque outdoor staircase.

Later, as a Feng Shui practitioner, it was clear we'd chosen a house that represented our inner lives at the time; we had chosen to disconnect from our old childhood experiences and foundation beliefs and create a fantasy world which, although alluring, because it was virtually unconnected to any foundation, produced a world which could only be temporary.

And so it was. When our adventure was over we returned to Montreal and picked up where we left off, this time renting a decaying building which had housed the Austrian Consulate until the Second World War. It was thirteen dark mysterious rooms hiding behind a locksmith's store, the sort of place that fit the old childhood patterns once more. There was a large closet under the stairs which became our receptacle for "stuff." Naturally this was in the area of the Feng Shui grid which represented our past experiences!

Edward House

In 1973, when Tilke was ten months old, we rashly bought a seventeen room, 1840 Federal Colonial house in Vermont. Though we could scarcely afford a down payment on the $15,000 asking price, it was, again, love at first sight. Back in 1840, the village had a railway station which brought people from New York and Boston to "take the waters" which bubbled from the nearby springs. Grand inns sprang up for the spa visitors.

A doctor had built our house for his patients. Sadly, after the First World War, the station was closed, the spa houses grew empty and the town's population moved away. By the time we saw the house, it had been virtually empty since 1929, save for an old caretaker. Rumor had it he and his wife died on the premises. Other rumors hinted darkly that neither of them had left.

The forlorn building we christened Edward House was a disaster. The back walls had settled into the ground, the roof leaked and a colony of mice had taken up residence. There was even a decomposing skunk in the cistern.

Imagination has always been my forte. Where others saw a neglected house almost beyond repair, I had visions of children and laughter and gardens of hollyhocks and roses, of peacocks calling from the lilac groves; balmy evenings on the porch and parties in the beautifully proportioned rooms. Besides, we'd never be able, or so we thought then, to afford a house like this in good condition.

It took us fifteen years. We spent countless weekends and holidays ripping out old plaster, sheet-rocking, painting, sanding floors, laying tiles. Tilke's first word was "mouse." Today, Edward House is a wonderful place filled with light and warmth, a place for children and animals and parties.

The Colonel's House

After this renovation we were ready for anything. In the mid-eighties we bought the house of a British colonel, built on the hillside in Montreal in 1900 as a summer cottage. As soon as the warm weather came, the Colonel and his family would climb in the horse-drawn buggy and set out for the stucco cottage on the hill, with its breathtaking view of the St. Lawrence River. When we bought the house it had, as the realtor pointed out "no curb appeal." It had been owned by a couple of Swiss scientists who spent most of the time in Switzerland, leaving their three young daughters at home with a nanny.

The steep front steps were rickety wood. Instead of flowers, the garden grew rusty tricycles. But the house clearly had good bones, and was set beautifully on the property, snuggled into the mountain at the back, in what Feng Shui calls the "belly of the dragon."

Armed with the confidence Edward House had given us, our new house was a piece of cake. In no time we'd replaced the wooden stairway with curving stone, planted an English perennial garden which poured fragrance and color either side as you ascended, added doors and a deck to the dark entrance, installed fountains, and a bay window. Then we restored the interior, keeping original woodwork, adding paint and wallpaper, until the original English cottage became a wonderful friendly sanctuary. Later, my friend Meredith donated a set of French doors to maximize the spectacular view from the living room balcony.

"It FEELS so good," friends told us when they visited us in Montreal and Vermont. For us, that was the key. Rooms had to feel inviting, friendly. Furniture must be comfortable, an invitation to children and the animals who were so much a part of our family life.

Feng Shui: gift of the heart

After my second book, *The Birth Report*, my childhood health weaknesses resurfaced. I developed heart valve problems and could no longer be on call day and night to accompany my clients in labor. It was time to change my life. I began renovations on my body, clearing out the clutter with living foods, rebuilding with more harmonious living patterns.

Illness isolates. By this time I had cut my workload significantly and was feeling sorry for myself. One morning David was reading *Esquire*. "Here, this sounds interesting… it's a writer's workshop at Bennington College in Southern Vermont." He passed me the magazine.

"Get drunk, get laid, get published" read the copy. It didn't sound like such a bad idea. I applied. I hadn't written a word of fiction in ten years. What had happened to the little girl curled up in her cubby house with her notebook?

My birthing involvement was work of which I shall always be proud, but it was time for a change. If you're going to write you'd better get started, I told myself. The problem was I didn't feel like a writer. I think it was Quentin Crisp who said something along the lines of, "It's no use complaining you were meant to be a ballet dancer after you've spent twenty years being a pig farmer, by then pigs are your style."

I empathized with that pig farmer.

To my great delight I was accepted into the Master of Fine Arts program in Creative Writing.

In that cozy campus of white wooden buildings I rediscovered the joy of writing fiction, placed on hold since my tree house days. There were only seven of us in the MFA program, most of us "mature" students. With a perfect blend of insight, kindness and expectation, our mentors, Nicholas Delbanco and Richard Elman midwived our dreams. Each of us in the program went on to have our work published.

I embarked on my first novel, *The Dreams of Zoo Animals*. Based on my Australian childhood, it explores the relationship of place and emotional development. As I began to write, old painful memories, blocked off for years, began to surface. For the next few years I phased out childbirth education and retreated.

My second novel, *The Loneliness of Angels*, was set in Montreal, and once more traced the interaction of place and emotion.

By this time the change in diet, pace and attitude had healed my heart, but with winter, as the thermometer plunged below zero, my old childhood bronchitis turned twice to pneumonia.

"You should get out of Montreal for the winter," my doctor suggested.

"David and I don't want to be separated."

"You might be separated permanently if you don't leave."

We looked at Sedona, Arizona, loved the red rocks and the sparkling dry air. We discovered a small house in the wilderness for sale. But there was a road permit required to cross National Forest Service land to the driveway. Application for the permit dragged on for months and in the meantime, I discovered Taos, New Mexico.

My friend Cynthia Drummond invited me and our friend Meredith Webster to attend a Native American ceremony at the Baca Ranch near Alamosa, Colorado. It was an extraordinary weekend of drumming, chanting and dancing in the shadow of great snowy mountains. On our return to Denver I met my dear friend, Peter Wollheim, who'd done the photographs for *The Birth Report*. We'd been commissioned to do a magazine article on a wolf sanctuary in southern Colorado.

Mission Wolf occupied two hundred acres and provided a refuge for wolves, both purebred and hybrid, raised in captivity. Most were abandoned after they proved inconvenient. They required more space and exercise. They jumped fences and howled. They behaved, in short, like wolves.

I slept in a small loft above the office, and in the early morning the wolves began to sing. I'll never forget the eerie beautiful song.

Next morning Peter and I happened to look at a map. Taos seemed an easy morning drive.

We set off to do an article on spec that I'd planned for years about the artist Georgia O'Keeffe who had first fallen in love with the southwest on a visit there.

Taos, New Mexico, almost 7,000 feet above sea level, nestles at the foot of the Sangre de Christo mountains on a high desert plane of fragrant sage. We parked on the main street which was thick with art galleries and tiny bookstores. Right away I felt at home.

As it turned out, Taos chose me, rather than the reverse. We'd finished the O'Keeffe research and were due in Denver that afternoon, when I met Sholan Chambers, a realtor who maintained she had the perfect writer's retreat.

The moment she unlocked the gate, I knew she was right. It was my place. Surrounded by a high latillo fence, the little adobe house had a separate studio perfect for writing. There were lilac bushes, apple trees... and the light was magical. The house, built in 1929 as part of the Mabel Dodge Lujan estate, needed work, a by now familiar sign that it was meant for me.

Socialite Mabel had moved to Taos, married pueblo Tewa, Tony Lujan and built a whimsical twenty two room house on the edge of the pueblo lands, inviting guests such as O'Keeffe, D.H. Lawrence, Carl Jung and Ansel Adams.

I arrived January 11, 1992, in a snowstorm, with my beloved borzoi, Bianca, after driving across the continent in four days. I shared the wheel with Adam, the son of my friend, Meredith. The final day of our drive we woke in San Jon, New Mexico, to a blizzard. By the time we stopped at Wild Oats Market in Santa Fe for something to eat, the road north to Taos was a whiteout. It was my turn to drive. A timid driver at the best of times, I could feel my heart thumping as I drove slowly through the mountain pass of the Rio Grande Gorge, keeping my eyes on the rapidly disappearing white line. Bianca, in the back seat, reached across and placed her elegant paw on my knee.

Just after we reached Taos they closed the road through the Gorge. We unlocked the door, exhausted. It was cold and dingy. No fire in the old woodstove. Not even firewood. A naked light bulb dangled wearily from its cord. Patches of plaster were crumbling around the electrical outlets.

I must confess, I thought I'd made a terrible mistake. Next morning, however, we bought gallons of plaster and whitewash. The sun came out, I walked Bianca out behind Mabel's to the cross painted by O'Keeffe in *Black Cross* (actually, the cross is white). The sage filled the incredibly crisp air with fragrance, the sky turned that unique New Mexican antique lavender and I knew I was home. When David and Tilke came for their first visit, the little house was clean and entrancing, just as I knew it could be, and I was writing full time.

The red circle of healing

Around this time, my dear friend, Marie-France LaHaye, called me in Taos from Montreal, and suggested I host a workshop on exploring our ability to develop intuition.

Marie-France is a wonderful psychic. "It won't be necessary to advertise for the workshop," she told me. "There will be twelve people." I trusted her implicitly, even when, one week before the workshop, the only people enrolled were my British cousin, Susan Blevins, my daughter, Tilke, and Susan's hairdresser, Christy. "Marie-France says there will be twelve," I maintained.

The day of the workshop there were eleven of us in my cozy little house. I gently chided Marie-France that she had mentioned twelve.

"But, of course there are twelve," she said in her delightful French-accented English. "Look, you can see the baby waiting to come in over Christy's head."

I couldn't see anything. I'm neither clairvoyant nor psychic.

"Yes, it's a little soul waiting to come in," she smiled. "You'll see."

Well, a few months after the workshop, which Marie-France called "The Red Circle of Healing," Christy announced her pregnancy.

I recall that at the workshop, Marie-France, channeling information for each of us present, told me, "This time next year, you Valmai, will be doing what I do."

What Marie-France did? Be a psychic? Well, this time my friend was way off target. I'd never had a psychic experience, never seen entities, heard voices or even wanted to. As it turned out, however, there was an element of truth to her reading.

At that workshop I met lovely, dynamic Patsy Cherney. Though familiar with some oriental design principles, I'd never heard the words,

Feng Shui, or if I had, they hadn't meant much to me. Patsy introduced me. It was as though I'd found my perfect medium.

I am grateful for the extraordinary gifts of Feng Shui, the ancient Chinese Art of Placement, both for the Fortunate Blessings which I enjoy daily and the privilege of guiding others to create their own Fortunate Blessings.

This is the story of my discoveries and those of my clients who, with courage and generosity, welcomed me into their houses and workplaces and their lives. It is my deepest wish to share with you these insights to help you explore your own.

Valmai Howe Elkins,
Sedona, Arizona.

Chapter One

The Origins of Feng Shui: The Myth, the Magic and the Mystery

If, like most of my clients, you've read several books on Feng Shui, you're probably familiar with the broad outlines of the subject. For those who are new to the ancient art a brief summary follows.

The words, Feng Shui, pronounced Fung Shway, mean "Wind and Water."

One of the earliest mentions of the term is preserved in a fourth century scroll which contains directions for locating the ideal grave site.

"The Chi travels by the wind and is stopped by the water's edge. The old ones guide it so it cannot disperse and move it so it cannot be still. It is therefore named wind and water."

History has it that 3,000 years ago, Fu Hsi, the Emperor of China, saw a tortoise emerge from the waters of the Lo River in northern China. As he meditated he had a sudden realization that the orderly markings on the tortoise shell were a code that presented the key to every single system in the entire universe. The combinations of solid and broken lines, he decided, symbolized each aspect of nature, wind and water, fire and earth, and every possible combination of the elements. Fu Hsi formulated the Lo Map, sometimes referred to as the "Magic Square" — a combination of eight trigrams of the nine cardinal numbers.

In the trigrams, unbroken lines represent Heaven or Yang energies, broken lines, Earth or Yin energies.

The *I Ching*, or Book of Changes, details the results of every combination of the possible 64 trigrams. Until 1200 BC, the information was passed on orally. In that year, scholars King Wen and the Duke of Chou produced a text based on a concept of a world in constant change, with humanity at the center, between Heaven and Earth. The oracle, studied by Confucious and Lao Tsu, was believed to hold the key of understanding to every human condition.

It is intriguing to note that while in 1953 Crick and Watson discovered the template for all life, the 64 codons of DNA, 3,000 years earlier the Chinese sages set down in the *I Ching* the template as they observed it in nature. In 1973, German philosopher Martin Schonberger put together the extraordinary correspondence: the absolute one to one equation of the 64 hexagrams of the *I Ching* and the 64 DNA codons. While the *I Ching* was supposedly put together from astute observation of nature together with highly developed intuition, and the DNA discoveries from our most advanced use of scientific technology, the conclusions were identical.

The Feng Shui Bagua

The grid of nine squares is referred to in Feng Shui as the "Bagua," an energetic map which can be applied to any and every location. The combinations of unbroken yang lines, with broken yin lines, are applied to areas of a dwelling or workplace which best represent certain activities. For example, the trigram for the area called Heaven is pure yang energy: three unbroken lines. The strong yin energy of Earth is represented by three broken lines. The Bagua is the basic tool of Feng Shui, The Art of Placement. The Bagua helps us to "diagnose" a room depending on the placement of each piece of furniture and object.

The Belly of The Dragon

The original Feng Shui practitioners were Taoist monks, geomancers who guarded their secrets and passed the tradition on with meticulous care. Working to choose auspicious burial and dwelling sites, they studied the land in minute detail: the position and shape of mountains, rivers, effect of wind and the placement of rocks.

From this they concluded that the best siting for a house was in the Belly of The Dragon, the dragon in China being a creature which brought many fortunate blessings.

The information was extremely practical. Ideally, your house would be located not on top of a mountain, where it could be swept by strong winds, nor at the bottom, where it could be flooded by strong waters, but in a gentle slope of the hillside, protected at back by the hill, or "dragon," with available water supply below. From this auspicious location you also could see anyone approaching, often referred to as the "Command Position."

As people moved from the rural areas to the cities, these basic principles were translated to the new urban environments. Instead of a mountain, you might have a tall building, tree or wall behind you. Roads represented waterways.

The Magic Square

Each number of the Bagua represents an area of our lives, based on the interpretation of broken and unbroken lines from the *I Ching*, a balance of yin and yang, male and female, assertive and receptive, outgoing and inward looking.

THE MAGIC SQUARE

4	9	2
3	5	7
8	1	6

Number One: the Life Journey

Located in the middle of the bottom of the square, "One" represents the beginning and the flow, referred to as "The Life Journey" and encompasses our choice of Career.

Number Two: Relationships

Located in the top right corner, "Two" represents our relationship with self and each other, including choice of life partner and business colleagues.

Number Three: Health and Family

Located in the middle of the left side, "Three" represents our relationship with our ancestors and traditions, our roots, including our connection to Mother Earth, our biological family and our extended global family. When these relationships are harmonious, optimum health — physical, spiritual and emotional — is favored.

Number Four: Fortunate Blessings

Top left, "Four" represents the sum total of harmony, creating our security, our material well being, our overall prosperity.

Number Five: Our Center of Unity

"Five" is the center of the grid, a neutral area known as the Tai Chi, complete harmony of yin and yang, dependent on harmony between the eight areas.

Number Six: Exchange of Service

Located bottom right, "Six" represents our ability to contribute to others, and our capacity to receive support in exchange.

Number Seven: the Creative Child

Mid-right, "Seven" relates to the child, the child we were, our actual children and all which is creative and playful.

Number Eight: Experience

Located bottom left, this area is commonly referred to as Knowledge or Contemplation. I choose the word Experience because our knowledge is produced from our experience. "Eight" is the sum total of every experience from birth on; the beliefs and values we have absorbed, the lessons we learn and the resultant insights. As we gain insight we are able to share and teach.

Number Nine: Illumination

Located mid-top, "Nine" represents illumination. When we are doing what we love and are traveling down our correct road we can both contribute and be recognized as our authentic selves.

This area is frequently referred to as Fame and Recognition, by-products of offering the world our authentic selves.

Which School is What?

If you've read several books on Feng Shui, you may be confused about how to apply the Bagua grid to your house and rooms. Some of your confusion is likely caused by the fact that there are several schools of Feng Shui. Each positions the Bagua differently.

The Compass School combines the use of the Lo Pan compass with astrology, divination and geomancy to determine your most auspicious directions.

In this school, the Bagua is calculated according to compass directions. Directions are correlated with your date of birth to produce a profile of your most and least auspicious directions and corresponding areas of your dwelling.

A second school is based on the work of Master Lin Yun. In 1986 he founded in Berkeley, California, the Yun Lin Temple of Black Sect Tantric Buddhism. Referred to as the Black Sect School, sometimes as Black Hat Sect, orientation of the Bagua is based on the idea that because the universe is holographic and changing, the Bagua is oriented from our point of energetic entry. Called also the Three Door Approach, you decide which is the main entrance and base the Bagua on that, repeating the calculation in each room. Your entry door is called the Mouth of Chi, the entrance where you welcome energy.

The Form School looks at the effect of land forms, shape of lot and floor plan, influence of surrounding structures and flow of Chi.

Another approach to Feng Shui appears more culturally specific. For most of us, the application of Seven Portents, which determine auspicious and inauspicious areas of a house according to location of energy, with names like Celestial Monad, Six Curses, and Five Ghosts may feel less accessible.

Flow of Chi: Your Chair is Alive!

Regardless of divergences in the various schools of Feng Shui, all approaches are based on the concept that everything on the planet is alive. Thousands of years before quantum physics, Feng Shui was based on this principle. While it's not difficult to accept that the worlds of humanity and those of the animal and plant kingdoms are connected, it's not generally assumed that the chair you sit on, the car you drive and the picture hanging on your wall are also alive.

Once we understand this, the basis of Feng Shui is clear and logical: We affect each other. The pile of old broken furniture hidden in our basement affects our lives!!!

You can visualize Chi as water... when you open your front door you welcome it into your house. From this point we want a harmonious flow room to room, neither a waterfall nor stagnation. Placement of furniture, doorways, kitchen islands, windows all influence the flow of Chi, as we'll discuss later.

The Elements

All schools of Feng Shui include the cycle of five elements: Water, Wood, Fire, Earth, Metal. Each element is represented by colors, shapes, materials and a corresponding area of the Bagua. For example, Number Three, the area of Health and Family is seen as the area of Wood and the season as Spring. The colors of new growth are greens and blues.

Each element nurtures another element and, in turn, is controlled. We give our plants (wood), water. Water is dammed by earth. This is a useful principle when we plan a harmonious room.

Balance of Yin and Yang

Balance of the two forces is integral to all the schools. The power of yin is often described as "feminine;" the moon, nurturing, receptive, dark, soft, intimate. The power of yang is often described as "masculine;" the sun, assertive, outgoing, bright, flamboyant, large. Each element of design can be interpreted in terms of yin and yang to create harmony in each room.

Discovering the Meaning of Numbers

I found the concepts of the flow of Chi, the balance of five elements and the harmony of yin and yang easy to understand. There are many excellent books which detail these concepts. You could think of these principles as the nuts and bolts of Feng Shui.

My understanding of the principles behind the Bagua was more elusive. I spent hours staring at the square of numbers and trigrams. Then one day I picked up a felt pen and began to draw each number carefully, concentrating on the actual strokes.

Here's what I discovered. If you'd like to try it, get a pencil, crayon or pen.

With your pen, form number one. You start at the top and make a line down the page. In the same way, the Life Journey comes from Heaven, the unseen world, a gift to us. Everything begins with this gift of life, the commencement of our personal odyssey.

To form number two you start within consciousness, form a half circle going out, bring it back in and complete the stroke by creating a base, moving out towards others. The moment we're born we enter relationship with self, then our mother, father, immediate family, those around us.

To form number three we draw two half circles, going from within to without and back, twice. In the same way, once we begin our relationships we become part of a family, those who have gone before us (above) and those who come afterwards (below). Our relationships nurture all aspects of our health.

For number four we start at Heaven and move towards Earth, then as we move the line out towards others, Heaven gives us another line. Surely, this is Fortunate Blessings.

To form number five we make a short line from Heaven towards Earth, then curve this out in a half circle, receiving. To complete the five we give to others from our highest consciousness, our spirituality. This represents perfect harmony.

In number six we accept the intentions and gifts from those around us, give back and once more receive. The circle at the bottom represents the cycle of giving. Truly this is service.

To form number seven we take our inner gifts granted from Heaven, express the energy, then bring it down to Earth; surely this is giving birth, either physically or metaphorically, our Creative Child.

Number eight is infinity, we repeat the two circles. Heaven and Earth, giving and receiving. This is the eternal cycle of our experience, knowledge, insight and wisdom.

When the eight areas are in harmony, we fill our potential and create number nine, formed by a cycle of exchange at the highest level of spirituality, past down to earth to benefit those around us. In return we are recognized for our authentic selves. This final, highest step is Illumination, also referred to as Recognition and Fame.

I was excited! In school, when I first discovered numbers, I'd been fascinated. I liked to draw them. But the teaching of arithmetic in Australian schools was guaranteed to snuff out any spark of excitement. As we droned the multiplication tables in sing-song voices I soon learned to leave the room in flights of imagination, my lips forming the sounds from habit only. Imagine if we had been taught the meaning of numbers!

I read everything I could get my hands on about Feng Shui and tried out the principles whenever I got the chance. Naturally, I started with my own environment. I applied the magic square to the houses we'd lived in and came up with some fascinating insights.

The former Austrian Consulate had featured a vast dark storage closet in Number Eight, the area of Experience. It was a receptacle for our "stuff." When it was full, literally to the ceiling, we closed the door. When we did manage to get the door open, our stuff fell on our heads, so we simply kept the door closed. Correspondingly, at that stage in our lives, David and I preferred not to examine our childhoods or past experiences, choosing to just barrel along into the future.

Finally, the dynamiting for a nearby subway caused the earth below the house to shift. One evening we came back from Edward House to find the ornamental ceiling of the hallway lying on the oak floor. When the ceiling to the room where I gave my birthing classes, and part of the ceiling over our bed followed suit, we knew it was time to move.

At that point another sort of ceiling was falling around our heads. We were going through a difficult period in our relationship, our experience had clogged and was backing up into our lives. The ceilings were the last straw.

Interestingly, in every house leading up to my heart attack, Number Three, the area of Health and Family contained a large staircase, including the outside steps at the tiny villa in Corfu. We roared up and down those staircases rushing from one thing to another, meetings, parties, work; up and down, floor to floor. Something was bound to give.

After I healed my heart we bought the Colonel's house and broke the pattern. It's as serene as they come, a sanctuary we were finally able to resonate with.

The Loft

Edward House took a while to figure out. For starters it had three wings and seventeen rooms. It's our oldest house, the one that's seen us through all our ups and downs. During the years I was sick, our Number Four, a loft above the kitchen shed, was so clogged with furniture and boxes from previous owners we hadn't even tried to penetrate it; there were, we thought, other more important things, like building a kitchen and getting the house solid. That clogged room was a metaphor for our Prosperity. We both worked hard, unbelievably hard. David had started his own publishing company and was working eighteen-hour days. I was working by day at the Catherine Booth Hospital, and four evenings a week teaching classes in our living room. Looking back I don't know how I managed the pace. I can only attribute it to youth and enthusiasm.

The night before Tilke was born I taught a class at The Booth. At 9:20 am the next morning she arrived, after just three hours of labor. Even that seemed to reflect the pace at which we were living! The same night, the physiotherapist who was supposed to fill in for me called my hospital room.

"I hate to ask you this," she began, "but my daughter had cosmetic surgery today and she needs me with her tonight. I wonder if you could just pop downstairs for the class, maybe tell them about your birth?"

What could I do? I finished breastfeeding Tilke, handed her to David, donned a lab coat and went downstairs to share the birth with my class.

There was no such thing as Maternity Leave in 1973. Tilke was born on Thursday. I was back teaching the following Monday. I wore Tilke in a front pack. Later we were lucky to have a delightful young Californian, Paula Williams, care for Tilke between my classes. I didn't have a car. At feeding times I'd jump in a taxi and rush home. Looking back, I saw how I shortchanged my baby and myself as well. Naturally if I'd known back then what I know now I would have made sure I'd had time out.

Getting back to that loft at Edward House, as soon as I embarked wholeheartedly on Feng Shui I knew we had to clear it out, yet we couldn't face it. We didn't even know what was in it. It was a dark ominous mass that stretched from the top of the wooden stairs into a dank and cobwebby infinity.

Every weekend I'd climb the stairs and mutter about our blocked Fortunate Blessings. At this point David had yet to be convinced of the powers of Feng Shui. Then one weekend we stayed in town. Great. I didn't have to deal with The Loft. Our area of Fortunate Blessings at the Colonel's house was a wonderful kitchen with a brick fireplace. Not so for Number Six, Service, which fell in my cluttered office. I spent two days throwing out outdated files, newspapers, old clippings and generally cleaning up.

Sure enough, along came Helpful People. That very weekend while we were in the city, Tilke and her friend Matt Power, with youthful energy, decided to take on the loft. When we arrived a week later the loft was empty. On the lawn beneath the window was a mountain of stuff; broken wooden shutters, battered oil lamps, a cracked china chamber pot, soiled letters of a soldier from the front; a button-up ladies' boot with no pair; a pillow which had obviously been the birthing place of generations of rodents. This represented our Fortunate Blessings. Other things were more redeemable and after a lawn sale and an enormous bonfire, right away our careers picked up. Not only that but suddenly we were able to address the challenge of The Deck, something that had been bothering me at the Montreal house.

The Deck

We discovered the Colonel's house in early October. Montreal was at its fall glory. We explored the sunny rooms, the kitchen with its warm brick wall. We opened the patio doors to the wooden deck. Below us stretched the world, or at least a spectacular view of the city extending all the way down to the river miles away, glowing with burnt oranges and crimson foliage. Nor was it one of those right-on-the-edge views. Our view was gently cushioned by giant maples and birches in a patch of woodland beneath a neighboring house higher up and out of our line of sight. Moreover, the handsome slate roof below us made our house feel completely tucked away and private. Nobody could look in any of our windows; we didn't even need curtains.

So enamored were we with the view we scarcely glanced at the decking beneath our feet.

It wasn't until we moved in that I began to notice it. It felt rotten and precarious.

That bothered me but we had other, more pressing concerns: replace the dangerous wooden front steps with stone, paint the inside. By the time the rest of the house was brought up to scratch the budget was at ebb tide.

That deck represented our Number Nine: Illumination. The moment we moved into the house our careers appeared to go into hibernation. It wasn't that we stopped working. No. They just didn't get the recognition we expected. My third novel, *Making Mother Immortal* was having a hard time of it. David's projects were similarly dormant.

"It's that wretched deck," I'd tell him. I hung a few Feng Shui toys out there, red flags, wind chimes. I replaced four rotting boards in the deck, hammering them in triumphantly. Our careers picked up for a month or so and then went dormant again.

I knew we had to deal with the rotting beams beneath the deck. David at this point was still not fully convinced of the effectiveness of Feng Shui.

"We HAVE to replace the deck," I told him.

One Thursday night he reluctantly agreed. We drove to the lumber yard and filled the back of the Explorer with treated one-by-six boards. That was the easy part.

The problem was that because the house was cut into the hillside there was no access to the deck except up those thirty two steps, then through the house. Not only did the new boards have to be carried in, but the old rotten ones had to be lugged out.

It took us two evenings to get the old wood out. Then we discovered we had to dig out the earth underneath them to install the new beams. It took us eight hours to manhandle the twenty-something buckets of earth through the house and down the stairs. Two weekends of hard work later, the new deck was finally in place, level, solid and secure feeling.

Two weeks after that, David's magazine won two awards. When the next readership studies came in he'd moved to the top. David was a convert. From that point on it was, "Just tell me what we need to do and I'll do it."

We've never looked back. The next week I was invited to do my first Feng Shui consultation. ༺༅༻

Chapter Two

The Case of The Back Door

*I*n the following chapters I'd like to take you with me on some of my more significant "cases."

To "solve" each case, I applied every principle of Feng Shui and added the ingredients of what I recognize as my particular strength; the intuition and eye of the detective, developed in that far-away Australian childhood.

For years I had helped friends decorate and prepare houses for sale. They seemed pleased and their houses usually sold, but I didn't think much about what I had done. It was fun, that was all.

Then one sticky hot day in Montreal, I was unloading some groceries from the car when a friend pulled up. It was Debbi, who ran the kennel where I boarded my dogs, a place where I knew they'd be well cared for as I traveled. She and her partner Marcello provided a convenient pick-up service and the moment they arrived, my dogs began to bark and wag their tails in joy. They couldn't wait to climb into the van and be off on an adventure of their own.

I hadn't seen Debbi for a while. I knew she was involved with Greyhound Rescue, finding foster homes for discarded racing dogs.

"Hi, Debbi, how's it going?"

Instead of her customary cheerfulness, Debbie gave me a worried look.

"Not so good. You know how I've always wanted to swim and work with wild dolphins? Well, I've got my chance down in Florida. And Marcello wants to sail around the world. We put the kennel up for sale, along came a buyer and I bought a house in Florida. Now the kennel sale's fallen through and I'm supposed to sign for the new house in a month. I don't know what I'm going to do."

Though I was distressed that the people my dogs loved were getting out of the pet boarding business, the words that popped out of my mouth were:"How would you feel if I came and took a look at the kennel. Maybe I could do some Feng Shui to help."

"I don't care what you do, as long as it works. I'm ready to try anything. When can you come?"

"How'd tomorrow afternoon be?"

"Terrific."

The lobby of the kennel was, as usual, friendly and attractive with big posters of their newest greyhounds up for adoption on the board.

At first glance everything looked about as attractive as you'd hope for. I wandered through the cattery where a handful of free-range cats lounged in the sun. All seemed well.

The grooming room was attractive, pink towels covering the tables.

At the back, the dogs began to bark and jump up as I walked between the rows of pens. Clean, uncluttered. Good Chi here too. Then a little voice somewhere inside me said, take a look at the back.

As I walked further to the rear of the building I felt as though I were "getting hotter," like Hide-and-Seek when you're about to find someone.

The moment I approached the back door I knew I was onto something. There were two doors, an inner and an outer one. I opened the first door. The area between the doors was dim and dingy. In a corner leaned a rusty hand lawnmower with some old dead leaves at its base. On the wall beside it were cobwebs. The outer door looked weary with its peeling paint and rusty hardware. Beyond this door stretched the field where they exercised the dogs. I knew this door was the clue.

Sure enough, when I applied the Bagua grid, it turned out to be the door of Number Four, Fortunate Blessings. This is frequently referred to as the "Wealth Corner."

As I see it, Fortunate Blessings encompasses the big picture of prosperity: If we're doing what we love to do, we are capable of making a true contribution to those around us. This will create harmonious and caring relationships, including those with all members of our family. This in turn creates health, creativity and the opportunity to be recognized for our unique qualities. When we have all of these qualities, money flows easily. The net result is Fortunate Blessings.

Debbi and Marcello's back door virtually said, "Our prosperity is being cut off by this rusty old lawnmower. There are cobwebs and dead leaves preventing this tired old door from opening. The energy is stagnant."

Problems in one area of the Bagua are never isolated. I knew I'd find constrictions elsewhere. Sure enough there they were in Number Six, a back room crammed with discarded objects and a disused desk with its back to the door. This indicated to me that the exchange of energy with the universe was as stagnant as the back door. Without flow in Number Six, everything to do with material prosperity will be handicapped. It didn't surprise me that the sale had fallen through. The reason they'd had the offer at all, I believe, stemmed from the high energy in the reception area, Number One.

Even here though, when I looked carefully, there were clues; cracked concrete outside, broken lights, grimy outer windows. In fact, every area of the Bagua revealed a clue.

Debbi, Marcello and I walked to the back door.

I said, "If I were to ask you, "Show me your vision of prosperity, is this where you'd take me?" I was only half-joking.

They burst out laughing. "Of course not!"

They were eager to make changes. We sat down and I outlined my very first plan of changes for someone else which I christened my "Recipe." I'd never heard the word applied to Feng Shui but it seemed to me that you couldn't just give a list. I could sense where the blockages had begun and how they'd progressed. The energy needed to be moved in logical progressions.

Debbi and Marcello ploughed in with customary enthusiasm.

"We'll do anything to sell this place fast."

That weekend Marcello's family came in to help do some clearing out, fixing, painting and rearranging.

By Monday the door was painted, the space was cleaned, junk was cleared away, old lights replaced, and a pair of guardian stone dogs, always good Chi, had been positioned by the front door. Finally, they listed their prosperity goals on a piece of paper, put it in an envelope and afixed it to the now spotless back door. Within two weeks a new potential buyer appeared, someone they had known for years and trusted. Two weeks after that the sale closed. Debbi set off for Florida and Marcello began to seriously plan his dream sailing trip of the South Pacific, something he'd wanted to do for years.

I was happy for my friends and returned to my novel. But in the following weeks my phone started to ring. Debbi had given my number to a slew of her friends.

"Debbi told us what happened with the kennel," they'd begin. "Could you come and do my house?" Or apartment? Or studio? Or office?

At first I wasn't sure I wanted to do this on a large scale. I needed to make myself very clear. So I said to whomever might be listening: Okay, Universe, I'm a writer. I have this great novel I'm working on. If this is what I'm meant to do, I'll do it, but the moment it doesn't help someone, I'm quitting.

The Universe Responds

On those first calls I'd pull up at the curb and sit in my car, feeling nervous. This was a big responsibility. What if I made a mistake about the flow of energy and its blockage points? I was affecting someone's life, so I'd better be good and sure I was accurate.

Don't Tell Me Anything

I think it was my childhood passion to be a detective that structured my consultations. Unencumbered by any knowledge of how a Feng Shui practitioner operated, I played it by ear. I didn't want to know anything about my client up front.

"Please don't tell me anything about yourself," I'd say as soon as anyone called and asked for a consultation. If Feng Shui really worked, the clues would all be waiting there for me to discover. If I were told ahead of time things such as, "We're having a health problem," or "Money's short," I was afraid my mind might jump into the old counseling mode from my days as a childbirth educator. This would be coming from me, not the environment. So I decided to go in cold. And if I called it wrong it was back to the novel.

Miraculously, each time I began knowing nothing about the person who lived there, not even how many people or what their relationships were, I'd find some clue that would lead me to the end of the ball of string. I always did the initial investigation on my own, then once I was sure of the diagnosis, I'd walk through the home or place of business with the person who'd called me in, describing what the environment was saying about them. Afterwards we'd sit down and I'd give a "reading," a detailed account of what the property, house and rooms indicated about their lives.

A reading might include something like this

"The placement of the painting in the entrance hall would indicate that at age seven there was conflict with the mother which led to the belief of being unable to support yourself doing what you love to do. The blocked door in the basement bathroom indicates difficulty with a creative project, and the position of the desk in the office would suggest that work is a struggle and there are problems with either cash flow, legal documents or an inheritance. The beautiful plants in the kitchen indicate generosity, taking care of others."

And so on. After a complete reading I would ask for comments on how accurate it had been.

When I heard the words, "It's absolutely correct." or "I'd say it's 100 percent," I was initially as astonished as my client.

But it's the next step that's always the most exciting. I'd suggest a formula of changes to unblock energy and, working over the next month or so, I kept in touch to see the results. They were truly amazing.

Health problems cleared up; new opportunities in work and relationships opened; money began to flow. But rarely without some clearing out.

Feng Shui Flu

Feng Shui is powerful. In the beginning, old conflicts, old issues presented themselves. Sometimes this meant a rocky period for my clients. It was as though in order for new energy to come in, anything that was holding the person back needed to be spring cleaned. Sometimes this was a physical "healing crisis." The person developed a cold or felt very tired or had disturbing dreams. My clients dubbed it "Feng Shui flu." Then the good stuff began to come in, often heralded by a shift in the nature of the dreams from disturbing to joyful and loving. It was fascinating.

Before long I was doing Feng Shui full time, spending as much time on follow-up phone calls as I had at the actual house or apartment.

All the books on Feng Shui that I had read focused on how our house affects us, vis a vis the architecture, the floor plan, location of doors and windows, colors of walls, placement of furniture, siting of toilets, stoves, sinks, desks and beds and so on. By placing auspicious items, the books suggested, we could enhance energy in the various areas of the Bagua. A typical suggestion might be that if you wish to improve health, place some healthy plants in Number Three. These cures get results in much the same way a shot of vitamins can perk up our physical energy. Then one unexpected snowy day when I felt tired and not as perceptive as usual, along came my breakthrough. 🐉

Chapter Three

The Case of The Old House
and The Dancer

*I*t was snowing lightly the day I arrived at Marie-Thérèse's home. I parked the car and instructed my new borzoi puppy, Daria, to chew her bone, not the upholstery. I'd wanted to leave her at home but she told me she would be much happier waiting in the car.

The apartment was in a high-end complex complete with pools, tennis courts, shopping center and health club. A vigilant doorman took the license number of my car and ushered me into seemingly miles of mirrored hallways and hushed elevators.

As usual, I had asked my client not to tell me anything about herself. This was important to me.

"As far as I'm concerned my clients are Snow White and the Seven Dwarves," I'd joke. "I don't want to know how many people live here or who they are."

Marie-Thérèse's entrance was tastefully decorated with expensive furnishings, carefully chosen artwork, lots of plants and big windows which on sunny days must have bathed the whole apartment in light. It was apparent that she had excellent energy for helping others.

She showed me the coat closet and went back to a telephone conversation.

"Think of me as a sort of friendly ghost," I'd suggested. "Just go ahead and do what you'd do normally. I'm going to snoop and creep and when I'm finished we can walk through and discuss it all." If the truth be known, I always consider anyone who invites a stranger into her or his house to snoop and creep rather brave!

As usual, I focused on finding the central clue. It had always happened before, the one small piece of evidence which invited me to unravel the secrets of what was really happening in my client's life. Without knowing quite why, I headed down a hallway to what was obviously the master bedroom, fine bed, puffy duvet, lovely linens and a view of the city.

My eyes were immediately drawn to a corner however. On the wall hung an oil painting of an old house. It was clearly the work of a talented artist. The wooden roof was sagging, the house in apparent decay. Snow covered part of the roof and the surrounding landscape of bare trees made me shiver. I'm not fond of snow, except perhaps a light fluffy dusting from six to midnight on Christmas Eve. A few feet from the painting was a piece of sculpture, a bronze of a young dancer, poised on one leg, the other stretched behind.

Suddenly I knew what was going on in Marie-Thérèse's life, the central theme, the challenge.

I must confess I was a little reluctant to tell her my findings. What if I were wrong? Don't be silly, I told myself, you didn't choose to do Feng Shui, it chose you. Either you have the gift or you don't. If you don't it's better to find out before you mess up someone's life. Following the clues, I proceeded to examine the details of each room. They added up.

When it was done I walked with Marie-Thérèse through each room and outlined the flow of Chi.

"Please don't give me any feedback until we finish the assessment," I asked of her. Once again I wanted to avoid receiving information that could influence the reading. The best thing a client can do is remain inscrutable!

Marie-Thérèse made tea. We sat at the kitchen table, piled high with books and papers. It was apparent from the "stuff" everywhere that her life was jammed full in every sense.

"This is an apartment ideal for learning and teaching," I began. "Any research you're doing would be well favored but right now an aspect of family and possibly of the circulatory system in the body is partly blocked. And it's as though career is at a standstill." I continued with my general findings, outlining the overall patterns. Then I plunged in.

"The central issue right now is in the area of relationship. There appear to be two relationships in focus. The first is represented by the painting in the bedroom of the old house in winter; the second by the bronze dancer. It is as though one relationship is decaying, the emotions frozen, while the second relationship is the dancer on one leg, poised in flight."

I finished, sipped my tea and looked at her expectantly. She was a strong and impressive woman. Right now she looked stunned. We sat there in silence. Outside, the snow continued to fall and the afternoon sky darkened. Then she said slowly.

"What you've said is absolutely accurate. I've been having a relationship for years with a man who's not available to marry me and it's really not going anywhere. He's much older than I am and now his health's going downhill. Then about six months ago I met a terrific younger man but it's as you said with the dancer, he's poised to fly off, he's not ready to commit.

"I keep going round and round the same old stuff in my mind, and you're right, I've got a problem with my circulation. Right now I can't concentrate on my career. I just want to get healthy and clear about where my relationships are going."

Together we put together a recipe of energy changing which included relocating the old house and the dancer.

Over the next three months Marie-Thérèse's life changed dramatically; opportunities opened in career, her health improved and men appeared out of the blue. The next time we spoke she sounded perky.

"I have all these men calling, asking me out," she told me, "But you know, right now I just want to get on with my work. I'm writing a book and have a publisher who's interested."

Marie-Thérèse is a wonderful woman whose considerable talents were unable to serve her fully because of energy blocks which, as for each one of us, slowly accumulated over many years. Once she began to remove these blocks, she started to realize and apply her power, both to help those around her and, in turn, to receive Fortunate Blessings herself.

Our Inner Blueprint

The Case of the Old House and the Dancer was so dramatic it made me think more deeply about what I was doing. The questions kept coming, especially that classic, "Which came first, the chicken or the egg?" Had Marie-Thérèse been affected by her choice of artwork, or had she unconsciously selected art which reflected what was going on in her life? And if this were so, then every tiny thing we choose to surround ourselves with tells a tale, expresses, if you will, our inner blueprint.

More important, why had she become enmeshed in unsatisfactory relationships? Why do any of us?

The answer to this, I believe, lies in the way in which our early beliefs and values are formed.

For example, if as a child, you watch your parents in an abusive relationship, this, like it or not, is your primary role model. Chances are, like so many of my clients, you've reproduced a similar relationship. Then you say to yourself, how come I'm not in a good relationship?

Not surprisingly perhaps, after my initial assessment, when I ask my clients to outline their goals, they'll say, "I'd like to have a good relationship."

But as we probe deeply they haven't a clear idea of what a good relationship actually is.

This is where the most important step of Feng Shui comes into play: See What You Have Created.

It was apparent from the books I'd read and from my own observations, that buildings AFFECT us. Now I became convinced that our homes and offices also REFLECT us.

I went home and snooped around my own house. The results confirmed my hypothesis.

Just one example: I've always loved the Henri Bougereau painting you often see now in poster shops, the one with a marvelous male angel tenderly transporting a young female angel through the clouds. Before my days of Feng Shui I had unknowingly hung the painting in the Illumination section of the area of the house which represented Relationship. As I reflected on it, I realized my marriage had taken a dramatic turn for the better at about the same time we moved into the Colonel's house and I hung the painting.

David and I have had twenty eight years of a marriage which spans the full spectrum of lows and highs. The first five years of our marriage were the most difficult; remember the clogged closets, the crammed and filthy loft, staircases of rushing family Chi, the rotting deck?

Early in our marriage, when we moved into the former home of the doomed Austrian Consulate our landlady offered us a pile of antique lithographs; murky browns and sepias. The theme was lonely moors and Highland bogs with an occasional mournful stag. They came with a bunch of Victorian oil paintings in tarnished gilt frames. Once more the themes were dark and gloomy, brooding women, anguished men, forlorn children. Looking back, the big question for me was, had the paintings affected us and produced difficulties, or had our energy dovetailed with those shadowy images? After all, we could have said, no thank you, to the landlady. She'd invited us to her house, a country estate, to collect the artwork. It wasn't as though they just appeared on our walls!

My conclusion was that we chose to hang the paintings because they resonated with our inner blueprints. They reflected perfectly our unexamined pasts, dim and murky. It was also interesting that when we decided to rent the house I was three months pregnant. Because of the locksmith's shop which had been added to the front of the grand old house, you had to walk through a long, narrow, poorly lit passage to reach the front door. The first night I held my childbirth classes in the two rooms we'd decorated with purple carpet, one of the women joked.

"We thought we'd got the wrong address. It's like you have to come in through this long narrow hall, like a cervix." The cervix is the name for the opening to the uterus!

David and I shared a peculiar lack of desire for self-understanding, locking away anything we found distasteful, a pattern we had both learned in childhood, doubtless a pattern our parents had learned in their respective childhoods and so on back for generations.

The result reminded me of the old-fashioned pressure cooker my mother used to cook with. She had to be careful to adjust the valve to let steam out. The one time I used it, I forgot to adjust the valve, the pressure built, the lid flew off and our lamb stew flew all over the nice white ceiling. On the surface, David and I were the perfect couple. We were loving, creative and we were immensely supportive of what poet, Rilke called our "artistic solitude." At least in theory.

Trouble was, with a young baby, two developing careers and a behemoth of a house, there isn't a whole lot of time for any solitude, artistic or otherwise.

Inevitably, if you haven't learned a way of dealing with conflicts, the pressure builds until it explodes. When this happened we were bewildered. We'd yell at each other, feel terrible and wonder why, when we loved each other so dearly. Later, my illness forced us to examine the way we dealt with conflict. And we moved house. The piles of garbage bags which contained items we no longer chose to live with, lined the sidewalk. Suddenly we wanted to get away from all those gloomy old lithographs and paintings. We followed the movers through the dark rooms, through the cervix and out into the light.

The moment we chose the Colonel's hillside house we went from darkness into the sun quite literally. No more Victorian gloom. It was in this house that our ideal was nurtured; a pair of angels soaring through the sky, tender and joyful. At this point we bought the Bougereau. Coincidence? I don't think so. ᦅᡟᢞ

Chapter Four

The Case of The Knight

From the moment we met I've always seen David as my knight, and he considers me his lady.

Recently, we drove five days from the east coast to the southwest on our annual winter migration, in two cars, he with Victoria our pot-bellied pig, Elizabeth his 13-year-old British bulldog and Teddy, the aging Pekinese; I, in the other car with Daria and Alyosha, our borzoi pups. If I had ever doubted it, this occasion proved David's knighthood to me once and for all.

It was day four. We'd driven ten hours through drenching rains and we were starving. When we stopped at a roadside café in Oklahoma the owner standing under a soaked and sagging awning told us, "Sorry, folks, there's no food, the rain's brought the roof down."

We eventually found a Cherokee Roadhouse, ate our meal and pushed on. Three hours later, crossing the Texas panhandle, I discovered I'd left my purse, a birthday present from my friend Meredith, at the roadhouse. I wailed to David on the CB, "Something terrible has happened. I've left my purse, you know the one with the little gorilla hanging from it, back at the restaurant. Everything's in it; my money, my driver's license, my credit card, insurance card, my passport, even our tickets to Australia." My parents had been ill and we were planning a visit.

We pulled off the road at a motel surrounded by stretches of short brown turf under a great cloudy gray sky. The highway curved into the horizon, the endless stream of trucks just turning on their lights.

"I'll go back," he said. I swear there was not a single note of rebuke. "We'll check you in here with the dogs and you can write your book review." Occasionally I review Australian novels for the Toronto *Globe and Mail* and the latest, of Murray Bail's wonderful novel, *Eucalyptus*, was due in three days' time.

"You can't. It will take six hours. You'll be exhausted."

"No I won't. I'll listen to my Tony Hillerman tapes."

My knight returned late that night with the purse. And he was in good spirits!

"There was a very nice girl on the cash. They'd found it under our table."

Of course everything was intact. Before we moved into the Colonel's house and had the urge to hang the angel where we did, the incident might have had a far different outcome. 🐉

Chapter Five

How Buildings Affect and
Reflect Us

Certainly I had discovered buildings which affected the people living in them in no uncertain way. The house with the big dark tree blocking the area concerned with health was contributing to the depression of the woman who lived there. That, in many ways was common sense. Yet the placement of the tree in her area of health and family dovetailed exactly with her early family history. Her mother had been alcoholic, her father had left the family when the children were small. Was it an accident that she was attracted to that particular house? I am convinced that it was not.

The cottage with the original main door boarded over was bound to stagnate vital Chi. Sure enough, the man who lived in it had been trying for most of his life to find something he loved to do. He'd wanted to be a photographer. His father had bullied him into the family business.

Now, as I looked for clues to the inner world, I was intrigued by how clearly the messages spoke.

Why Do We Decorate?

I've always been interested in the seemingly universal need to decorate. In my travels I've been fortunate enough to spend time with the Australian Aborigines, live on the Greek island of Corfu, spend time on an island off Hong Kong and roam freely through European villages and the Pueblos of the American Southwest. From the most primitive lean-to, to the grandest celebrity mansion, there is a concern with decoration in one way or another.

Why does one person choose a painting of a beautiful flower garden and another a desolate bombed city? My experience as a Feng Shui "detective" indicates to me that we choose according to our past experience and our inner state.

Based on this hypothesis, a happy childhood will be reflected in choice of paintings, placement of furnishings. That's exactly what I've found. Paintings of happy children, flowers, abstracts with beautiful colors, animals very often appear in harmonious homes. Just what you'd expect, right? The fascinating thing is that my experience with Feng Shui has shown me time and again that it works the other way too. Create the happy atmosphere in the outside world and the inner world begins to change as well.

I had been practicing Feng Shui for close to two years but I knew no other Feng Shui practitioners. I figured it was time to connect with others in my new profession. I wrote away for brochures on workshops. The one I selected was held at a macrobiotic retreat center in New York State, given by a recognized Feng Shui Master. It was to be a week's session.

I mailed in my registration fee and eagerly anticipated my trip, arranging to have Daria cared for by friends.

Then Monday morning a week before I was to leave, my phone rang. It was the secretary at the Feng Shui course. "You've registered for the course that started today. I'm just calling to see if you're coming."

I almost fell off my chair. "I have it marked on my calendar for next week." I began to think quickly. My friends who had offered to take Daria were out of town until next week. David was in New York.

"I've made a terrible mistake but I can drive down this afternoon if I can bring my dog. She's very well-behaved." I must have sounded quite bizarre to the poor woman!

"I'm sorry we don't permit dogs."

"Then I can't come."

I was terribly disappointed.

A few evenings later I told my friend Addy Hyman what had happened. Addy is an extraordinary person. In her eighties, she's one of the youngest people I've ever met, full of wonder and sparkling energy. Visually impaired since her teens, she cycles, skis, hikes and works full-time as a psychotherapist. Her clients adore her. So do I. Every Wednesday we get together. Sometimes I read to her and we discuss what we've read, on other evenings we simply relax and see what comes up. On one memorable occasion we produced an audiotape. This is how it happened.

For many years, I've taught a course on Obstetrics at McGill University's School of Physical and Occupational Therapy. One of the techniques I discuss with students helps women feel comfortable with their bodies, with their sensuality. Women who enjoy their own sensuality as well as sexuality are more likely, I have found, to move freely with the sensations of labor. Belly-dancing is about as sensual as you can find.

As part of the workshop I have my students belly-dance, using Lebanese music. I was due to give that particular session on a Thursday. Wednesday, just before I went to Addy's house I couldn't find my usual tape.

"Addy," I said. "You don't happen to have a tape of belly-dancing music do you?" I explained why I needed it.

"I don't." She thought for a few moments. "Why don't we make one?"

She disappeared into a back room. When she returned to the living room she had her tape deck, a plastic waste bin and a selection of bells.

"I'll drum and we can both use the bells."

I jumped into the spirit of the game.

"I'll chant."

Apart from the muffled laughter at the end as we collapsed on top of each other, the tape, believe it or not, sounded authentic. When I played it to David he didn't appear to suspect. Nor did my students. Addy and I still howl over that tape.

On this particular Wednesday evening however, I was feeling down. How could I have mistaken the dates of the Feng Shui workshop?

"Addy, I made a horrible mistake," I told her. "You know how much I was looking forward to the Feng Shui course? I missed it."

She listened carefully as I described what had happened. Then, with all her wisdom she said,

"You know Valmai, it wasn't a mistake. You don't make mistakes like that. You're not meant to be at that workshop. I think you're meant to develop your intuitive approach more before you find out how other people do it."

I believe she was right. When the following year, I did enroll in a course, I'd learned to fully trust my intuition, my ability to sniff out clues.

At The Western School of Feng Shui, north of San Diego, I simply relaxed and had fun. I enjoyed meeting others who were practicing. It was great to compare notes.

Terah Kathryn Collins, author of the excellent book, *The Western Guide to Feng Shui*, was a clear and accessible teacher. She was also a warm, caring person with a lively sense of humor.

I honed my knowledge of the five elements, yin and yang and the application of the Bagua. I walked in the crisp sea air and found a wonderful living food restaurant. I laughed a lot with a group of new-found friends. We were each encouraged to develop our own particular style as a practitioner. At the end of the program my personal approach of "Feng Shui detective" felt validated. Terah jokingly referred to me as the "bloodhound of the Feng Shui world."

In the next two cases the major "clues" lay in childhood. Because childhood is the beginning of our journey, our NUMBER ONE, I was not surprised to find evidence of constricted energy in the corresponding areas of each house. ⚘

Chapter Six

The Case of The Three Horses

My client had said on the phone, "I won't be there when you arrive. I have some things to do. Just go right in."

The house was at the end of a winding, well-treed lane, with only an occasional glimpse of any dwelling. It was a warm spring day with all those wonderful smells of the ocean; salt, sea grass and sunbaked sand. I pulled off the sandy track and into the parking area. The gulls didn't bother to move from the garage roof beside the copper dolphin weathervane.

I walked to the edge of the concrete parking area, and the land dropped abruptly. Below stretched a glorious expanse of wind-tossed ocean, and across the bay, big mountains the shape of breasts.

My hair blew across my eyes. I love wind and cliffs and being high above an ocean. I felt like twirling and shrieking. But instead I walked slowly towards a tall wooden archway beside the garage. Except for an intriguing glimpse of wooden turret, the house was hidden from view.

On one side of the wooden walkway was an ornamental address plate, number 63.

Two big pots, one terra-cotta, one blue ceramic stood beside it. On the other side was another large pot. Each was filled with smooth earth. On the wooden railing were two window boxes, empty except for a gardening trowel. Behind the boxes were three black plastic pots, stacked together.

The wooden walkway led to a small Japanese-style gate. I stepped into a charming courtyard with a glimpse of deep blue ocean. Seven rose trees and a honeysuckle grew against the wall of the garage. The courtyard was filled with bird feeders and a wind-chime tinkled in a budding apple tree.

The garage was connected to the house only by an oriental-style trellis. When I pushed open the door it felt blocked. Sure enough, behind it was a storage rack of boxes. Among the boxes of children's toys I noticed an open box of small nails. A wooden cricket bat leaned against the boxes.

A screen door with two small tears in it was stacked against the wall. Behind it were boards and a pointed shovel.

I paused in the corner by the door to examine a curious art collection made of eight square frames, different colors, set at an angle across an abstract of multi-angled colored shapes.

I was beginning to get the pattern of energy in this house.

Down the hill curved a wooden staircase. As I descended, the cliff dropped away and I noticed boulders and old wind bleached tree trunks scattered down the slope. By the side of the house leaned a stray wooden door and it was apparent from the piles of wood that something was under construction.

At the front of the house was a square of lawn with a child's brightly colored jungle gym and pots of healthy blue and yellow pansies.

I stepped through another wooden gate onto the windswept hillside. Piled among the seagrass were an old chair, a box of congealed cat litter with a scoop, and a stack of old boards with rusty nails sticking out. On this side, too, the cliff dropped away to the sea.

The house, perched on the edge of the cliff, was bordered in front by two levels of wooden decking; what a view! The upper deck with its vertical wooden railings was painted driftwood gray, the lower deck, redwood.

My first impression as I opened the front door was of light and warmth and, in spite of the expanse of sky and sea, of intimacy. Built on several levels, each room was filled with color and comfortable furniture, healthy plants and colorful artwork, much of it clearly the work of a child.

Adjacent to the entry, in Number One, Life Journey, was a small bathroom, designed for children. On one side stood a child-height mirror, one which would not reflect the face of even the shortest adult.

The shower curtain was a map of the world. The children's room contained two bunk beds and many of their cheerful paintings. A closet just beside the front door concealed the washer-dryer.

The glass dining room table held a big basket of many-colored candles. The kitchen smelled of herbs and spices, with two racks of well-sharpened knives attached to wall magnets. You could tell that someone who lived here enjoyed cooking. I stood at the sink and noticed the gulls across the waves.

The living room occupied one whole side of the house, with glass patio doors leading onto the deck. In the corner was a healthy jade plant, a pair of drums and a hanging crystal. It was apparent that my client had some knowledge of Feng Shui. A cozy brick fireplace contained niches filled with candles. I could imagine this room on a chilly evening, the sound of the sea below. Hanging in the window was a pretty antique birdcage which held a big blue glass bird with four smaller birds — a bird family.

In the master bedroom, a king size oriental-style bed was flanked on one side with a ladder holding a large vigorous plant. When I opened the door to the closet it closed against the main door.

In the basement was one of the most whimsical bathrooms I've seen, with a staircase leading up to the toilet, a little throne. I climbed the steps and peered through the window behind the toilet. Five boards lay on top of the trellis to the garage. Outside the bathroom, another door which led to an office, was blocked by colorful children's chairs: red, yellow and blue.

The basement playroom featured another huge healthy jade plant and many candles, colorful artwork. I paused in the center of the room, feeling by now my familiar "alert," the sense that I'd struck the mother-lode of clues. Sure enough, in one corner, along the baseboard I bent to examine a small patch where the plaster had bubbled, the way it does when there's a slow leak. I touched the wall; it felt cool. I admired a big antique wooden cradle a few feet away. On a shelf above the cradle stood three china horses; a chestnut brown one standing head raised, a slightly smaller black one bending forward, hooves delicately outstretched, and a smaller dark horse in a similar position, which reminded me of a curtseying circus pony. On the opposite wall was an oil painting of a sunlit staircase descending into mysterious golden green vegetation.

I knew what was happening in my client's life.

As I returned to the kitchen I heard her open the front door and call to me. As I requested, she remained inscrutable as we walked through each area of her house and property while I explained what I'd noticed.

We returned to the living room and she poured water in blue glasses which caught the afternoon sunlight. From our sofa we overlooked the mountains across the bay, the ones I'd christened to myself, the Breasts.

"Natasha," I said, "this is a beautiful, magical home ideal for children. However, for the adult, there is constriction which results from childhood difficulty." She leaned forward and cupped her chin in her hand. I continued, "There are two patterns happening here. Inside the house there is intimacy, very feminine intuitive energy. There is the capacity to care for others, to mother those around you and generate good fortune. There's the capacity to manage money. Yet because of the placement of the house with its landslide formation down the cliff, it's as though whatever is accumulated falls away and it's a constant struggle, especially with prosperity and relationship. It's a little like two steps forward, one step back."

Her eyes opened wider.

"The theme of the house is Illumination. When we are doing what we love, "following our bliss," we develop a strong core of confidence which allows us to develop our inner light. As the light grows, we radiate this into the world which in turn, honors us for our authentic gifts. This is generally referred to as success, recognition and fame."

I went on to explain my assessment in detail.

In Natasha's house there were two definite patterns. For the real children, the life journey energy flowed as freely and playfully as anyone could possibly wish, with a strong core and plenty of light. Truly, as the shower curtain indicated, the world was their oyster. That child-height bathroom mirror indicated that for the adult, childhood had been a different story.

"An aspect of the mother is empty," I continued. "and there is pain associated with the father.

"Yang, the masculine force tends to overpower the yin, or feminine. It is as though the child has been suppressed, pushed down. While there is a strong core of survival, there is old obstruction which limits relationship with the yang, or male force. Yang relationships tend to go over the edge, to be cut away. They are precipitous. You're very strong at the core, but there is a lack of supportive energy coming in. I would imagine that you have many good friends, but even so, you're giving more than you're bringing in." Then I asked, "Could you tell me what happened when you were five years old?"

Tears welled in Natasha's eyes. We waited a moment, then she began.

"I grew up in Rumania. My parents had two girls and six boys. My older sister was the light of my father's eyes. When she was thirteen and I was five, she got very sick. My father said to me, 'Natasha, go in with your sister and pray to God to save her.' I went in and she was breathing very strangely. She died while I was in the room. I was terrified. After that my parents didn't pay much attention to me. My mother told me they hadn't wanted me and she'd actually tried to abort me. My father and my brothers bullied me. My mother and I were treated like their servants. I still have all this anger about them." She took a gulp of water and continued, "The father of my two daughters and I separated two years after we bought this house. He turned very nasty and kidnapped the children. He kept them eleven months. Every day I prayed and surrounded them with protection. I got my children back, but it's been a struggle to sort things out. Now we share custody and it's getting better, at least it's civil, but he's not reliable with child support. I have a good job but I don't earn as much as some of the other people in my field. It's exactly like you said, the money just falls away. I'm tired of struggling. You're right, I don't feel I'm supported."

For the next hour I outlined a 'recipe' of changes, each change carefully structured to open up the energy in a way which would be manageable. It's rather like the child's game, Pick Up Sticks. You spill a can full of long wooden or plastic sticks. Using your fingers or another stick, you have to pick up each stick without moving the other sticks. Selection of the first step is crucial. From here we move on, slowly going deeper as the more superficial energy is moved.

Natasha's house represented her completely. Her naturally buoyant spirit had managed to create beautiful things; a loving environment for her children, loving friendships and a creative career. Like her house, she clung to the edge, appreciating the wildness and beauty of nature. While a house on the edge of a steep drop-off is too difficult for many people it matched Natasha's energy pattern. The trick was to preserve this natural wildness and connection with the elements but make sure her pattern was supported. The difference between exhilarating and precipitous was here, quite literally, the edge of a cliff.

It was time to balance yin and yang. The challenge of a house set with its back to a cliff was considerable. It is the reverse of the desirable "belly of the dragon." The big tree trunks in the "landslide" formation indicated the dropping away of the male, as Natasha had described. Eventually she would correct this by terracing, retaining walls and wooden decking. For now, we came up with a plan of using a balance of the five elements to "hold" the energy, which could be described as a waterfall. Each small piece of energy which was draining support would be carefully unblocked — doors which did not open fully, piles of debris, doors that went nowhere and gave neither protection nor opportunity. Objects both sharp and cutting were either removed or carefully stored.

In the same way, the wooden railings of the decks needed to be made solid and protective. We decided that the least expensive way would be to use blue canvas awning, woven between the railings. Then, instead of dropping down the cliff, the eye would go beyond to the very yin shaped mountains. Plantings of yellow flowers in boxes and Natasha's big jade plant also strengthened the area.

Of twelve steps, the last two were the deepest, most difficult. These would probably not be reached for a month or more. I suggested she release the five glass birds from the cage. She decided to get rid of the cage itself and use the stand to hang a healthy plant.

Finally it was time for the three horses; the chestnut yang and the two black, subservient yin, which represented precisely Natasha's early family relationships. Natasha took them into the woods, thanked them, blessed them and freed not only the horses but the blockages of her childhood as well.

When we spoke next she told me, "An interesting thing has happened. A few nights ago I had the first loving dreams I've ever had of my family. It was wonderful. And I was able to look at my parents with compassion and understand that they did their best, after all they were probably treated the same way by their parents."

Many, many of my clients report unusual dreams as soon as they begin the changes. It makes sense. As we begin to unblock, before we become aware of the movement of energy, our unconscious begins to process change, frequently producing a shift from old nightmares to new dreams of love and harmony. Naturally nightmares are disturbing. It's important to recognize that this is part of a "healing crisis." The intensity of this period appears directly proportional to the extent of old blockages.

Natasha called about six weeks after our initial consultation. "I have some wonderful news," she began. "Since I finished the first four steps in my recipe, something amazing has happened. I've had hemorrhoid itching for eight years and I've tried to heal it in every which way, everything from homeopathy to cortisone. The cortisone would clear it up, but the moment I stopped using it the itching would come right back. When it was really bad, sometimes I'd be up all night scratching 'til I was bleeding." She paused. I could feel her excitement. "The itching's gone. It stopped the moment I finished clearing out the garage. I feel like I've let go of all my old anger at my family. My brothers' behavior used to irritate me constantly. I feel differently about them now."

Chapter Seven

The Case of The Toy Monkey

"**I**'d like you to come out and take a look at my place." The voice on the phone was a woman's.

We set a date and, as usual, I said, "Please don't tell me anything about yourself until after the reading."

"Fine," she replied. Her voice sounded completely neutral.

The property appeared deserted. It was an unusual design. Clearly a great deal of thought had gone into the arrangement of four long low buildings opening into a central courtyard. The white clapboard buildings were attractive and well-built, surrounded by mature maple trees and fine landscaping.

I knocked on the door. After a few moments a tall red-haired woman appeared.

"Hi, I'm on the phone, you go ahead and let me know if you need anything."

"Thanks, I'll come in when I've finished."

As usual I began with the grounds. The day was cold and clear. The first leaves were beginning to turn crimson.

At first glance everything seemed in order. Following a hunch I headed off to explore the grounds. Some distance from the house, in a small planting of trees, I discovered my first clue. This was a property of several well-tended acres. Yet, here, in the shade of the trees was a pile of broken glass bottles by the look of them. On such a well-tended property, why hadn't it been cleared away?

As I opened the door to the main residence, I was confronted by a clothes rack with some T-shirts drying on it. Nothing too odd about that, there had been rain a few days before, but on the wall above the rack was an interesting piece of art. It was mixed media. Pasted on colored paper was an arrangement of those styrofoam "peanuts" used for packing fragile objects. The peanuts had been fashioned into the letters of the alphabet, weaving up and down across the paper. A, B, C, the following letters were scrambled. Toward the other side of the picture were peanuts pasted to resemble crossbones, like the ones on the classic pirate flag, The Jolly Roger.

Aha!

I walked further into the room. Resting on an antique cabinet comprised of twenty four tiny boxes was a toy monkey, clearly quite old. It was one of those plush monkeys with a little red jacket you associate with performing monkeys, the ones you see in old movies perched beside an organ grinder. On its head was a little cap. I stood there and looked at it. Something about its expression disturbed me. It looked as though it expected to be punished and was doing its best to ingratiate itself. It looked, in short, servile.

I moved on into the living room. On either side of a large TV set was an elegant oriental vase. On top of the set was a wicker hamper. I opened the lid and lifted out a book entitled *The Terrible Eek*. On the cover a child screamed, mouth wide, wide open, presumably at the terrible Eek, whatever that could be! The pattern in the house was forming in an unmistakable way.

I finished my work in the main house and crossed the courtyard to the building opposite. Although everything was clean and orderly, the rooms felt somehow disused and dark. On the living room wall hung an oil painting of a New England house in winter; white with gables. On impulse, I crossed the room and examined the books in the wooden bookcase. There it was! I lifted out Nathaniel Hawthorne's book, *The House of The Seven Gables*. Inside the cover were the words: "In a brooding old New England house live the last remnants of a once proud family haunted for generations by an ancient blood curse."

I flipped through the book and it fell open at page 144. There was a black and white illustration of a monkey similar to the toy monkey in the main house, same servile expression, its hand outstretched. I read the words carefully. "He had a monkey on his shoulder... the monkey took off its bonnet and made personal application to individuals, holding out his small black palm, and otherwise plainly signifying his excessive desire for whatever filthy lucre might happen to be in anybody's pocket... the prying and crafty glance that showed him ready to grip at every miserable advantage. Take this monkey, just as he was, in short, and you could desire no better image of the Mammon of copper coin, symbolizing the grossest form of the love of money. Doubtless, more than one New Englander passed by and threw a look at the monkey and went on, without imagining how nearly his own moral condition was here exemplified."

By the time I returned to Vanessa's kitchen I was sure of the pattern. Let's examine the clues:

The pile of broken glass on the property indicated to me that the integrity of the family had been shattered, causing extensive pain. This would logically predispose to health issues. The placement of the laundry in the hall was unexpected. It would be more appropriate to have it in the utility room, the kitchen or sunroom.

ABC's are the earliest building blocks of a child's logical learning, indeed they are used as a metaphor for precisely this. The scrambling of the letters, together with the apparent crossbones indicated to me that something had happened at an early age to disturb this basic development, to kill the spirit, if you like.

The toy monkey on the antique boxes represented the child, trained to perform to gain approval and avoid rejection. The twenty four boxes, adding up to Number Six, the number of Service, indicated to me that the earliest support, that of the parents, had manipulated the child.

The two fine vases either side of the television represented a partnership which, to the public, appeared strong. The partnership thrived on appearances. However, for the child, beneath the surface lurked the "terrible eek"... a secret family life the public did not see.

The New England house in the snow indicated to me that there was frozen emotion associated with the family and childhood. This energetic pattern was picked up in *The House of The Seven Gables*. With its exact replica of the toy monkey, it was apparent that the family that owned or inhabited the house had wealth, but this was perceived as somehow disgusting; associated with guilt and revulsion which resulted in manipulation of the child.

As we talked, Vanessa confirmed the pattern. She and her brother, who occasionally shared the house, were children of parents who inherited great wealth from an enterprise that gave them no joy. The number of the boxes beneath the toy monkey corresponded to the age at which she began her years of therapy. Currently she was in the process of examining the past, healing, washing, as it were, the dirty laundry, the placement of which had alerted me that here was a clue.

Not surprisingly, Vanessa's relationship with money was filled with contradictions. It represented both security and manipulation. She had difficulty handling her bank and trust accounts, taxes and cash flow. And for years she had attempted unsuccessfully to deal with a major health problem that left her unable to do the work she enjoyed.

"The thing that amazes me," she said. "Is that book, *The House of The Seven Gables.* I haven't even read it. I bought all the books in that room at a sale!" As often happens with Feng Shui, the origin of a given item is not important. What is important is that it is there whether the occupant of the premises is aware of it or not.

The recipe of energy changes I suggested began with a complete clearing of broken glass on the property. This was followed, at carefully timed intervals, with a cleaning out and getting rid of clutter and old family objects piled into the fourth building. As the energy began to move, Vanessa took a fresh look at all the artwork. She decided to give away some, relocate other pieces.

Simply by being aware of the energy which surrounded her, she was able to begin to address old issues of family conflict.

"My parents are coming for a visit next month. It's my brother's birthday. Usually we fight so much I can't stand it."

After the visit I called to ask how she was.

"You won't believe it. We actually behaved in a civilized way. It's the first time we haven't had some big argument. It wasn't perfect, but it sure beats anything we've ever had before."

Over the next year, as she processed the material coming up, she and her parents had several breakthroughs, not without confrontation and difficulty. But these became less frequent. Vanessa's health issues have improved, she is working with several approaches to physical and emotional healing, and she is beginning to have fun.

The most deep-grounded blockage was in her relationship with money. She spent too much, then postponed dealing with the consequences. However, as she completed the changes in her house, this also began to change, to the point where she is now both managing the money which has always represented those early childhood values and has also gone on to open up new ways of bringing in money, using her creative talents.

Chapter Eight

Family Feng Shui: The Case of The Gloomy Castle

Sometimes our Number One or Life Journey appears to be going along smoothly, then suddenly we run into a situation which, if we use awareness, can reveal insights about a difficulty we have created for ourselves.

While I was in the southwest, my daughter, Tilke, then attending the Boston Museum School of Fine Art, called one Sunday morning. She sounded depressed. Normally she is energetic and enthusiastic.

"I feel sort of trapped, here," she told me in a dispirited voice.

She was only a few months into her first term, living in the apartment of a house owned by a friend's aunt. At first it had sounded wonderful; a few blocks from Harvard Square in a safe area, an easy bus ride to the Museum.

"Tell me about your apartment in detail," I suggested.

"It's at the back of an old triplex here in Cambridge. Dave (a friend) has the top bedroom. The living room and kitchen are in the middle, we share them. And my bedroom and study are in the basement."

"What color are the walls?"

"White."

"The ceiling?"

"White."

"The floor?"

"White tiles."

"Windows?"

"Two little ones near the ceiling."

"Doors?"

"There's a door to the main house and I can hear my landlady talking to her husband, so I put a bookcase in front of the door."

"Which direction is your head when you sleep?"

"West, I think."

"What's on your walls?"

"Two paintings of castles and a landscape."

"Tell me about the landscape?"

"Sort of a moor in winter."

Now, in Feng Shui, the balance of five elements is basic to harmony. As we discussed earlier, the elements, water, wood, fire, earth and metal both nourish and control each other. For example, water nourishes wood which provides fuel for fire. Earth is formed from the ashes of the fire and from the earth come minerals and other forms of metal, which in turn, hold water. Conversely, water puts out fire which melts metal which cuts wood which digs earth which in turn dams water. Each element is represented by a range of shapes and colors.

White represents the element of metal. When there is an excess of metal, wood is diminished. Like an axe, the wood is cut. Wood represents health and vitality. It was apparent that Tilke's vitality was being drained by an excess of metal. Moreover, her choice of castles, one in Number One, the other in Number Six, indicated that she felt trapped, both in her career and in her exchanges with those around her. Castles were built as fortresses, most contain dungeons used to confine prisoners. While the same castles, in another pattern of energy might have indicated protection, these two, reinforced by deserted snowy moors, definitely represented a prison. Moreover, their stones added more metal to the white room. Interestingly, Tilke had selected the artwork of castles several weeks after moving into her metal-dominated space... an inner signal that things were becoming gloomy.

The placement of her bed with its head to the west further reduced her energies. The west, after all, is the area we associate with the sinking of the sun, time to sleep. This would be excellent for someone experiencing too much energy, but in my daughter's situation it was simply making her feelings of sluggishness worse.

"No wonder you're feeling trapped," I exclaimed. "You're in prison... all this metal and stone walls!"

I suggested she begin by relocating her bed with its head to the east, bringing in the energy of sunrise. This was bound to speed up her energies. Because it was a student rental she was not permitted to paint the walls. Her landlady was not too keen about hanging anything or changing things at all. To balance the excess of metal, we decided to remove the castle paintings and replace them with her own paintings to be done in reds and oranges, the colors of fire. Peach and pink sheets and some red pillows on her bed balanced the metal.

She decided to place her blue bottle collection on the window sill relating to her health energies, to bring in the blue of wood and water (glass represents water, blue, wood). In place of the lonely moor she hung a cheerful photo of herself with her friends. Finally she removed the bookcase blocking the door and activated the energies here with a small lead crystal. To further enhance the Chi, she hung her red and orange origami dragon mobile, made for her by her friend, Matt, from the ceiling.

As soon as she turned her bed she phoned to say she was feeling more energetic. "The moment I took down the castles I felt a change in the energies, Mummy," she told me. "And I found a red pillowcase in a thrift shop."

Two weeks later she told me, "I want you to know that Feng Shui is 100 percent accurate. I painted the red and pink and orange paintings we talked about and hung them where the castles were. I feel terrific and, guess what, Matt's invited me to visit him in Salzburg, Austria, and I'm going to write a travel piece."

Once more I pondered the chicken and egg question. Was her choice of rental as haphazard as it appeared? Or had some part of my daughter resonated with the "prison." When we discussed this in length she confirmed the latter.

She loves the country, especially New England where, at Edward House, then at St. Paul's School in New Hampshire, and later at Middlebury College, she could hike and enjoy natural beauty and solitude.

While she was excited to try Boston, leaving her beloved countryside was a wrench. Even before Matt's aunt offered her the apartment, she was feeling imprisoned. Hence her choice of artwork.

The white room represented for her the draining effect of the city on her vitality.

She successfully completed her year in Boston, made friends and turned it into a valuable experience. But the following year she moved on to complete her Master of Fine Arts at Bennington College, once

more in her beloved Vermont countryside, balancing this with frequent
weekends in New York, a recipe which has proved ideal. ❧

Chapter Nine

The Case of The Empty Refrigerator

The life of a Feng Shui practitioner, I firmly believe, must reflect a basic harmony. By the time I began to counsel professionally, I could honestly say that my life was filled each day with Many Fortunate Blessings. It felt harmonious. However, harmony is not a static state. It requires on-going awareness and vigilance! With all this fenging and shui-ing I wondered why my own energies were feeling depleted. Normally I, like Tilke, have high energy and a positive outlook. I enjoy my life.

At this time I was spending part of the winter in Sedona, Arizona, a glorious place of spectacular red rock views, crisp sunny days and cool nights with brilliant stars. David was away on the east coast on business and I could feel my energy waning. I described my feeling to Tilke the next time she called from Boston. She questioned me.

"What's in your fridge?"

"Not a whole lot, you know I don't feel like eating when I'm alone."

David and I have a good arrangement. He loves to cook and I love to eat. When he's not around in Taos or Montreal, I simply go out to eat. There's a great vegetarian cafeteria not far from our home in Montreal, and in Taos I can walk a few blocks for a choice of wonderful cafes. In Sedona, however, at the hideaway we call The Dragon Farm, we're out in the wilderness, bordered by thousands of acres of National Forest Service Land, reached only by three quarters of a mile of a rough dirt road that crosses several dry creek beds, called washes. It's not a place where you run out on the spur of the moment for a nice latte or a burrito, indeed after a storm the road is scarcely passable.

When David's here he likes to shop and cook and I'm probably the world's most appreciative audience.

"What's in your fridge, go and describe it to me." My daughter was relentless.

I crossed to the kitchen and opened the door of the big white refrigerator.

"Hmm. Teddy's eye drops." Teddy is our Pekinese. "And there's a jug of aloe vera and a bag of miso for soup but it's a bit dried up... and Victoria's almonds and raisins." Victoria is our eight-year-old black pot-bellied pig. It would be unpardonable to eat her favorite snack.

"Is that all?" My daughter sounded stern.

"There's some wilted celery and Daddy's collection of mustards," I said defiantly.

"Oh, I see. Tell me, Mummy, which area of the house your fridge is in."

I was silent. Then I answered, "Fortunate Blessings. Oh."

"You will promise me that tomorrow you will make a list of everything you like to eat and then you will get in your car and drive to Mount Hope in Cottonwood and buy everything on your list. And then you will come home and put the food in your fridge and you will eat it. Promise."

What could I do? She had, after all, trashed her castles.

Within days I felt a whole lot better, my phone was ringing with friends. I called Tilke to thank her for her clever Feng Shui analysis!

It appeared to be the season for family Feng Shui tune-ups. Shortly after I returned to Montreal, David's publishing business ran into problems with cash flow. Normally we are both blessed with abundance. This was unusual.

David is a firm believer in the joys of moving furniture. Indeed, as I mentioned earlier, we spent our first date rearranging the furniture in his house. He was eager to pinpoint the problem and start heaving things around.

"The money in the business is going out almost as fast as it's coming in," he complained. I had already Feng Shui'd his office and given a talk to his wonderful employees. Many of them went home and used some of the principles in their homes.

When I checked each area of the office I could find no drastic change. As in every home and office, things get moved and clutter accumulates. We did a little clearing out but the problem continued.

"I wonder if it has anything to do with the new office," he said thoughtfully.

He had taken a small area in a nearby building. It was here that he planned to finish writing his book of short stories, *Relative Exposures,* co-authored with his friend, Torben Schioler.

Since I'd looked at the space initially and selected the colors with him, I hadn't been in there. It was his private lair.

"Has anything changed over there?"

"Well, France, our accountant has moved into the room beside me. It was a bigger space than the one she had at the main office."

"Hmmm. Let's take a look."

The next afternoon I examined the offices. They were bright and colorful, the furniture was correctly placed. When I'd checked the space initially, only one of the rooms, David's, was occupied.

France's office was neat and orderly, sparsely furnished.

My thought process went something like this:

David is choosing to spend less time on the magazine side of his business and more doing his personal writing. He's taken a separate office. But the accountant is right there beside him. She's the accountant for the magazine. What happens when she operates from his personal writing space?

It suddenly became clear. David was concerned that if he weren't on location, the company would suffer. He'd relocated the money to his office. Moreover, he'd positioned her in his area of Fortunate Blessings. What he'd created was an unstable arrangement. The business had "lost" its accountant and David was unable to escape the financial pressures of the company and take time out.

France was happy to have me Feng Shui the office. While she was at lunch, I took a close look at the room. On impulse, I crossed the room and sat at her desk. It's a good thing I did.

The view was entirely different! From the door, the view from the window revealed fine old stone buildings with nice proportions and stone gargoyles. Now, however, my view was of a metal fire escape.

The picture came together. France's office was in the Fortunate Blessings area, associated with the element Fire. Did we really want a fire escape here? Moreover the escape represented a waterfall putting out whatever fire managed to survive.

Since we could hardly move the fire escape, this was clearly a situation for a "cure," one of the processes you've probably read about and wondered just how hanging a lead crystal or positioning a mirror can correct a problem.

Objects such as mirrors and crystals activate sluggish energy. We have to be careful precisely what we choose to activate. Cures also may use a balancing of the five elements, controlling an excess of one element with the introduction or strengthening of another.

In France's office we needed to dam the waterfall. We selected earth toned curtains. To feed the fire element, we brought in healthy plants, the wood element, including jade, the traditional, "money plant."

As in each case I've worked on, there were other minor adjustments as well. A connection needed to be made between the main office and the fortunes of David's literary enterprise. This was done by means of a logo on the front door.

Within a week or two, finances began to become more stable. David went on to complete his book. Harmony returned. 🪱🐛

Chapter Ten

Feng Shui in Business: The Case of The Corporate Saint

*R*ight after the incident in David's office, I began to have a run of commercial clients. One of the first was a marketing company in an elegant glass-sheathed high rise. As with my residential clients, I asked that they not tell me anything about the business until after the reading.

The company occupied a whole floor. I entered a vast reception area carpeted in thick dark gray, the receptionist positioned directly across from double glass entrance doors. From her position, it was clear that she probably wouldn't stay with the company long, the energies were coming at her too forcefully.

The Chi of this particular company roared down a long hallway which led from the elevator, through the glass entrance doors and flooded the reception area. I was not surprised when the president later confirmed that receptionists didn't stay long; they'd had several in the past eighteen months.

The offices which opened on the side hallways were small and orderly. However, three of the desks in the area of Health and Family were not in Command Position, indicating that there would be more sick leave than usual. Inevitably this would also weaken the health of the business.

The president's corner office commanded a spectacular view from the floor to ceiling windows.

However, we need to be careful about views. In this office, I could feel the energy being pulled across the floor and out the window. When I looked down there was an abrupt fall of fifteen floors to the street below. I stepped back quickly, feeling a slight vertigo. The large, impressive desk was positioned in Command Position but the back was to the window, causing energy to "leak," with a resulting lack of support for the president. As this office formed the cornerstone of Fortunate Blessings, it was clear that the finances needed shoring up.

I examined the details. Sure enough, there was the clue. On the wall in the area of Relationship was a gold framed oil painting of a cliff overlooking white-capped waves. Perched right on the edge of the cliff was a flimsy wooden house that looked as though a strong wind might blow it over the edge at any moment. It reminded me of E. Annie Proulx's delightful novel, *The Shipping News*.

I knew instantly that there were difficulties with staff. The Fortunate Blessings in a company are not so much the clients but the employees. These are the "Helpful People" of any business.

From the sharp visual drop and the rickety house I knew that the profits of the company were shaky and that this was the result of issues relating to staff.

This was confirmed by three major patterns of energy. The Conference Room, located in the area of Illumination, faced a brick wall, quite literally, indicating that the company would experience difficulty in getting its reputation out there. The other corner office was as bright and spacious as the president's, it belonged to the chief financial officer. There were healthy plants, photos of smiling wife and children. And there was something else. Another clue. In the Fortunate Blessings area of his office hung a painting of a saint, the hooded, brown-robed variety. This struck me as odd. Businesses, unless they are more than usually philanthropic, as a rule have little in common with the vows of sainthood which include poverty. The CFO's office was in the area of Relationship; the saint hung in the Fortunate Blessings area. This clearly presented some contradictions.

Further down the hallway the jigsaw puzzle came together. At the end of the hall, beside a spacious media room was a closed door. I opened it quite unprepared for the sight of two rows of tiny cubicles crowded into an area about a quarter the size of the reception area in the front office.

Not only that, the people crowded in the cubicles faced their desks with their backs to the door. Also, the view had been completely obliterated by heavy shelving and screening. An adjacent lunchroom had no windows, just metal tables, a microwave and a sink, with white walls and ceiling. My reading was complete.

"The placement of the desks in the first area indicates difficulties with the health of the employees and consequently the health of the business. The president's office indicates, from the placement of the painting of the house on the cliff and the sheer drop from the windows behind the desk, that profits are shaky right now. The conference room, which represents the reputation of the business, is literally up against a brick wall." I paused. "In the other corner office, the placement of the saint would indicate a conflict of interests regarding money and this is affecting relationships. The area of Helpful People is the room full of tele-marketers. Most of them have their backs to the door indicating both lack of support from the company and resultant lack of profits generated here. This, together with the health problem I've already mentioned and the whites and metals of the lunchroom, is causing further health difficulties and staff turnover."

The president looked at me. I couldn't tell what she was thinking. Then she nodded her head.

"You're absolutely right. We haven't gone a week without someone being sick and I'm feeling so stressed out it's affecting my relationships at home. And it's funny you mentioned the office with the saint. Since we've moved to this location, "X" has seemed to have lost his edge. In fact, he's giving information away instead of charging for it! And I know we should do something about the tele-marketers. We call it the bullpen."

She was eager to begin the recipe of suggestions. Three months later I checked in with her. She sounded much happier.

"We've made all the changes and you'll never guess what happened. "X" refused to move his saint. Actually he's left the company. It was all quite friendly. He said he needed to move on to something else." She went on, "And everyone's health has improved. We've put a mural in the lunchroom and the number of sick days has dropped right down. I'm feeling a whole lot better about things myself. Even my children notice the difference."

"How are your profits?"

"Terrific. Things are going so well we're expanding."

I recalled the corporate saint a few months later when I did Feng Shui for a friend's gallery in Taos, New Mexico. Susan Wilder Fine Art is one of the most attractive galleries in Taos. Located on historic Kit Carson Street, it's warm and inviting. Partners Susan Bossenberry and Rob Wilder curate a collection of New Mexican art, both traditional and contemporary, with encouraging support for young artists. In addition, they've created a gallery that makes you feel genuinely welcome. When I'm in Taos I like to pop in and bask in the warmth they've created and their openings are among my favorite events.

When you enter the gallery, Kira, Susan's Russian wolfhound — given my passion for the borzoi how could I not like the gallery? — rises elegantly to meet you. It's rather like walking into a living room; there's a welcoming fireplace, carefully selected antique furniture and, of course, the paintings.

Susan and Rob had recently moved from a gallery on the upper level of the historic Taos Plaza to the new location, a vastly superior and more visible one. Unless you really investigated you could easily miss the doorway to the former location. However, profits weren't as high as expected. They invited me in to check the Feng Shui.

The area of Fortunate Blessings was located in a small room of contemporary artists with a door to the parking lot. Clearly this was weakening Chi. Moreover, the door was painted white. As Fortunate Blessings is represented by the fire element, I suggested they repaint the door inside and out a lovely southwest pink, acknowledging that prosperity is the result of relationships with the clients. Under the central area of the gallery, I discovered a basement clogged with "stuff." They agreed to clear this of anything no longer necessary. In addition, they relocated landscapes of snowy scenes which had been positioned in the Life journey area.

There is nothing wrong with snowy landscapes, although personally, after those prolonged horribly cold Montreal winters, I am not a fan of winter. But the placement of these paintings in an area whose energy thrived on the flow of water was literally freezing the Chi!

Susan and Rob made the changes quickly. The profits rose steadily throughout the summer and fall until they had increased significantly from the previous year on the Plaza. Then in early winter I spoke to Susan.

"How's it going?"

"It's stopped. Things just suddenly went flat and I can't imagine why this has happened. "

"Describe what's in the room near the back door."

As she described the display I couldn't help smiling... in delight...

because there was something that could be done immediately to increase sales.

"We have a display of lovely carved wooden saints by one of our local sculptors," she told me.

"Susan, what vow does a saint take? That's right, poverty. Do you want a vow of poverty in your Fortunate Blessings area?"

She has a delightful laugh.

"Unless you want to give away all your worldly goods, you might like to relocate the saints."

We laughed together.

A week later the saints were relocated and the sales again began to climb. They've never looked back! Recently Susan was interviewed about the gallery and the history of art in Taos. The resulting Associated Press article has appeared in newspapers all over the country.

Chapter Eleven

Home Business: The Case of The Hammock

The home business has become a fact of the nineties. It's a liberating concept; you get up in the morning and instead of bracing yourself for the traffic you sip your tea in the garden, walk the dog, play with your children. After a leisurely breakfast with your spouse you head into your home office and work for a few hours until it's time to water the garden, have a snack, take a walk. After lunch you work 'til the kids come in from school. Sounds appealing, doesn't it?

While it's a wonderful concept that works just fine for many people, sometimes the patterns of work and family life can produce unique challenges. I had worked several times with Aphro and Raphael on both their home and office. Recently they'd moved to another city where, in order to spend more time with their young family, they each had an office in the house.

One evening Aphro called: "There are a few things here we need help with. Could you come up?"

The timing wasn't quite right for an out of town trip, so I suggested they Fax me the plans of the property and house and we could do a phone consultation.

"It won't be as detailed as on-location, but I have a feeling we'll pick up something."

"That sounds great. This is a rental and we'll be moving soon but we'd still like you to see if there's anything that can be done." I didn't ask her what the problem was, I wanted to discover it for myself.

The plans arrived a few minutes after I hung up and I studied them carefully at once, focusing on the energy patterns. By the time she called the next day I was pretty sure what the problem was and how to fix it.

"Aphro, we've got two distinct patterns of energy in your house. Your family life and relationship are doing just fine, you're relaxing and spending time with each other and the kids. The problem is with your business. Everything's set up to bring in great opportunities. You've got lots of help coming in from the Universe. Your creative energies are juicy. It looks as though the deal's about to go through then it just seems to wilt.

An image flashed into my mind. I grinned. "You know, Aphro, it's rather like an erection. We're all ready, then at the last moment sometimes things wilt!" She laughed. I continued, "On your property, you have a nice hammock between two trees in the area of Relationship. That's good. It's a great place to take it easy, relax with the kids. The problem is that because the house is situated sideways on the property, that hammock is directly adjacent to the Prosperity area of the house and affects it. When we apply this to your business we see that this will affect the profits. Deals come in, they look great, then just as they're about to close they lose momentum and don't come through. Let me put it another way. If I were to say to you, Aphro, show me the vision for your company, you'd show me that hammock."

"The hammock's out of there!" she said at once.

"There's another thing. Your Career area is represented by a closet and your utility room, also by that black slate stairway down into the garage. Energy is clogging in the closet, churning in the utility room and leaking down the steps."

"Oh no," I thought our Career area was the entrance. "We keep our garbage in that closet!"

Fortunately she and Raphael are great at making changes. They replaced the hammock with a line on which they hung red, yellow and blue flags. The movement of the wind would create prosperity for everyone living — and working — on the property and would serve relationships equally well.

They relocated the garbage, balanced the energy in the utility room and corrected the leaking.

The business perked up right away! 🐉

Chapter Twelve

The Case of The Empty Corral

*E*ach of the nine areas of the Bagua is related to the others. As we have discussed, in order to enjoy the full cornucopia of Fortunate Blessings, each of the nine areas needs to be strong and harmonious. It's not simply a matter of hanging a crystal in your Number Four area to mitigate a perceived difficulty. Though this should bring movement in prosperity — you might have an unexpected windfall or opportunity — in order to create prosperity consistently, each area needs to be fine-tuned to work with every other.

As I approached Vivian's property I could see, in the back left area, behind a row of trees, a horse corral. Nothing unusual about that, many people in this area of New England kept horses. But something wasn't quite normal. There was a light breeze blowing, yet I couldn't smell the distinctive horse aroma. I unlatched the gate and walked towards the corral. By the gate, eleven concrete blocks were strewn, with no apparent purpose. The water buckets were empty and there was not a horse in sight. No fresh manure. It was obvious that the horse or horses had left the corral some time ago.

At the back of the house the swimming pool glinted a serene turquoise. I paused to admire a pair of dragons curved around a pair of large ceramic green pots; twin dragons, one either side of the diving board. But although it was midsummer, the pots were empty. On the opposite side of the pool a big old wagon wheel leaned against the wall. On close inspection, several of the cogs were detached from the rim.

The entrance hall, with its formal black and white marble squares, featured a collection of interesting prints; medieval knights and ladies.

The living room was in the area of Number Eight, Experience. In the Number Eight area of the room was an antique clock — stopped at twenty to nine.

As I moved from one room to another, through tasteful antiques and shelves of books, I noticed several more antique clocks, each with the hands frozen. Then, in a small study, I paused to examine some paintings, stacked in a cupboard. They were disturbing, to say the least; skeletons writhed in apparent agony. Books on the Civil War and more knights and ladies filled in the missing pieces of my puzzle, together with several pots of aloe vera.

I never know ahead of time who lives in a house. But in this house, although the closets held male clothing and several rooms were clearly a man's study and library, it felt as though the yang energy had "left the corral." Yin and yang had been harmonious, the yang protecting the yin, with much love and passion; the knight and his lady. But something associated with much internal pain and suffering, a "civil war" had terminated their love. Since then, time had frozen, energies were in the past. While some healing was in process, it was as though the life journey was frozen.

It was a big house and the reading had taken longer than expected. Outside, it was growing dark. When Vivian generously invited me to dinner, I accepted gratefully, not looking forward to a meal alone at my hotel. As we ate, she told me the whole story.

"My husband and I had all sorts of plans, but we never kept horses. The month we moved to this house his doctors diagnosed cancer."

She had nursed him through the agonizing progression of his illness, until his death several years ago. The knight and his lady were torn apart, the yang energy or "horse" had left the corral. The twin dragon pots remained empty, the clocks silent. The energy in the house felt very still.

Slowly, as Vivian embarked on her Recipe, the energy once more began to move. A year later, while her relationship with her husband was still fresh and deeply honored, she began to move forward once more, taking pleasure in new interests. ༺༻

Chapter Thirteen

The Case of
The Sleeping Gardener

Mark invited me to Feng Shui his house and as usual, I asked him not to tell me anything about himself until I completed my initial assessment.

It was a lovely old property, one of the area's original houses, well set in the "belly of the dragon" on an acre of exceptionally beautiful landscaping. Flower gardens glowed with irises and bluebells, bordering a velvety lawn, unusual in the arid climate. Every square inch of the property was carefully groomed. Not much to do here, I thought to myself, I wonder why he called me in. Maybe just out of curiosity.

Relationship contained a meditation garden of St. Francis feeding the birds. Unlike the corporate saints in Fortunate Blessings, this was entirely auspicious, indicating generosity of spirit, kindness and caring in relationships with others, with the ability to nurture the vulnerable. This could possibly be the energy of a healer. The area of Enlightenment was protected by a hedge of thick native trees, indicating, not surprisingly, that rather than seek recognition in the outer world, there was a turning inwards at this time. Fortunate Blessings was similarly sheltered. However, there was in this area a small statue, one of those terra-cotta figures seated, knees drawn up under the chin, head covered by a pointed Mexican straw hat. Clearly the "gardener" was taking a siesta.

I had found my key clue.

The Health and Family area was a riot of bluebells. But as I bent down to smell the flowers I glimpsed something partly concealed by a rock. It was a small pottery snake, broken in two. The remainder of the property held no clues. It was a well-groomed sanctuary from the busy road on the other side of the tall hedges.

When I entered the house, although it was impeccably clean, light and tastefully furnished, the energy felt curiously still. I was drawn to the area of Health and Family of the kitchen... a sunny plant window over the sink. On the glass shelves fitted into the window stood a vase of four porcupine quills, three cactus plants, a wooden block which sheathed a collection of kitchen knives and a round fish bowl of plants with a jagged piece of glass missing.

My suspicions, drawn from the pottery snake, were confirmed. But as the smallest detail adds to the jigsaw puzzle, I continued with my journey through every room of the house. In the living room I stopped in front of the fireplace, in the area of Health and Family. Above it hung a lovely Vermont winter landscape. In the fireplace — it was spring and the days already warm — was a spiky cactus.

The placement of the desk in the office was back-to-the-door. A silver-sheathed pocket knife lay in the Relationship area of the handsome wooden desk.

At the end of my assessment, Mark and I sat down on the sunny front porch.

"This is a beautiful property, Mark," I began. "It's an ideal place to nurture anything to do with self-knowledge. It would be perfect as a place to sift through experiences and gain understanding from them. There's enormous potential in both Career and Creativity but right now it would appear that this is your time to withdraw from the outside world for a while. You're more concerned about self-enlightenment than with success and recognition."

Mark was listening carefully.

"But the placement of the terracotta gardener would indicate that right now, an aspect of prosperity, is dormant. It's a little puzzling. The energy here relates to money, but it's not a major concern. It's simply dormant.

"The placement of the broken pottery snake, together with the quills and cactus and knives in the kitchen window indicate possible health problems, maybe surgery or even the departure of a close relative. The snowy scene over the fireplace would possibly indicate frozen emotion or grieving."

I was watching his face carefully as we talked, trying to be as gentle as possible. He was silent, his face a mask.

"Hmmm," was all he said. After a few minutes he began to talk. "The year before I bought this house I lost every single member of my fam-

ily. My sister died of cancer, then my father died. Then my brother sui-
cided. I nursed my mother through terminal cancer. I used to be a chi-
ropractor, but after she died I gave up my practice and bought this house
with my inheritance. That was three years ago. I've been living here ever
since like a hermit, just dealing with death. A few months ago I decided it was time to go out into the world again. You're right, my prosperity's literally been sleeping... I've just decided to sell the house and
move to another state."

"So this place has been your sanctuary?"

"Yes." He smiled suddenly. "Actually that's the name of the house."

Mark chose to throw out the sleeping gardener. Over the next weeks
he repaired the snake and relocated the cacti to an outside patio, replacing them and the quills and knives with a big wooden bowl filled with
lush fruit: mangoes, pineapple, grapes. He discarded the broken fish bowl
and relocated the snow scene, made up the fireplace with paper and
logs, turned his desk so that he could see whoever entered, and kept
fresh flowers in the living room.

He also rearranged the Life Journey area. Three pieces of furniture
were back to the door. Shortly after he moved them into Command
Position, he called.

"This place feels totally different! My cleaning woman couldn't
believe it. She thought I'd done something like paint it but all I did was
move the furniture."

Shortly after, he moved to another city and enrolled in a course
which offered a newly developed approach to healing.

Chapter Fourteen

Our Fragile Relationships: The Case of The Convent Door

*O*ne of the primary reasons you might be considering the services of a Feng Shui practitioner is to improve the relationships already in your life or to attract a new relationship, perhaps an intimate one. In some ways I view this as the most challenging aspect of the Bagua. It seems that in order to bring in a positive romantic relationship, the sort of life mate so many of my clients are searching for, every other area of the Bagua must first be in order. It makes sense. Until we are aware of what we have created from our past experience, especially from childhood, we risk attracting the sort of relationship we'd rather avoid.

Until we're doing what we love to do, accessing our creativity and having fun, until we are making a contribution to those around us, we're less likely to be recognized for our authentic selves. Until this happens, our Fortunate Blessings won't run on all cylinders.

While we all want quick fixes, my experience indicates that, while occasionally after a Feng Shui "recipe" a client will phone and say, "You won't believe what's happened. I met this gorgeous man/woman...," in most cases this turns out to be not so much their ideal partner but a sort of Feng Shui "appetizer" while the deeper changes are occurring.

Nick is a case in point. He had been divorced two years when he called me in to Feng Shui both his home and office. He'd decided to cover every base. Deeply attached to his two young sons who spent five days a week with their mother, the clues in his sleek city condo indicated isolation. In the Relationship area of his bedroom was an oil painting of a young man alone on a windswept beach, a steep sand dune rising behind him, great white capped waves churning in front.

In the corner of Fortunate Blessings was a Paris street scene in the rain. People with umbrellas hurrying down the street in pairs; except for one figure, a young woman who stood alone, facing the viewer.

In the Relationship area of the house, which happened to be his study, was another painting, a small oil of a winding street. Set in a stone wall was the gateway to what looked like a convent.

Though tastefully decorated, the entrance to the condo, in the area of Career/Life Journey, featured an antique grandfather clock, the hands frozen at one fifty. In the kitchen in the area of Health and Family was another small antique clock, the hands frozen in an almost identical position. It was uncanny.

"Nick, the energy here would indicate that while there is great potential for creativity and Fortunate Blessings, something in your life journey to do with health or family has stopped. From the placement and position of the clock in the hall and the one in the kitchen, this would appear to concern intimate relationships. Is it possible that the child has been isolated in an institution with feelings of abandonment and that those feelings still exist?" With no reaction from Nick, I continued, "There is the possibility that when someone becomes close, that relationship will be severed in order to avoid abandonment."

When I come to the end of a reading, I usually wait a few moments then say something like, "Would you like to comment on the reading?"

But Nick didn't seem to want to talk at all. He simply shrugged. Had I made a mistake? Mis-read the signs? I began to feel uneasy.

Most clients are eager to tell me about themselves. Some, however prefer to just confirm the accuracy without giving me details. Either way, the important thing is that the person recognizes him or herself from the outer clues. And once this is acknowledged, we can begin to change the energy patterns.

Just as I figured Nick would rather not discuss himself, he leaned forward, propped his chin on his hand and met my eyes for the first time. "What you've just said sort of shocks me. It actually gives me the chills. My mother died when I was four years old and my father dumped me in an orphanage, one of those parochial places you read about where they mistreat the kids. I can still remember my mother, she really loved me. When she died, you're right, I felt completely abandoned. My dad would visit me only a couple of times a year.

"I've never had any close friends, I'm a stockbroker and I've always enjoyed my work. I like to work hard. When I met my wife it was love at first sight, but I guess I've never really learned how to relate to someone. She kept telling me I was cold. She left me for another man. The worst part is she got the kids."

His story fit the clues precisely.

These clues in our environment don't pop up overnight. It takes a lifetime to produce an energy blueprint. And, of course, deeply ingrained patterns won't disappear in a weekend. Nor should they! I've learned that it's essential to caution my clients to go slowly. I even try to spell out the timing of each step. Like a gourmet recipe, timing — and the right order — is crucial to the end result. If you just bung in eggs and flour and spices and shove it in the oven, chances are you'll get a culinary chaos. It's the same with Feng Shui. Even the smallest change is charged with great energy.

The changes Nick and I agreed on were worked out very carefully in what I call my "Energy Recipe." To begin with I select the step which is the end of the ball of string, energetically speaking. Then my client waits a day or two, in some cases three or four days, before going on to the next step. The moment one step is taken he or she immediately notices changes.

Generally the first step involves a clearing of old garbage. Images from the past surface, sometimes in the form of dreams. Feelings follow: hurt, sadness, anger. As the clearing occurs along come what I've called Out of The Blue's (OOB).

What is a typical OOB? Frequently it's a phone call or chance meeting with someone from the past, often someone you may have gone to school with or had a relationship with. It's usually an opportunity to recognize and resolve an issue related to the energy you're clearing.

In Nick's case, within forty eight hours of his first step, a girl he'd once dated called him.

"She was married to someone else and was passing through town," he told me. "And for some reason she hunted me down and called. We went out to dinner together and I apologized. You see we really liked each other, she was very sweet to me and I guess I got scared about the attachment and abandonment thing. I just stopped calling her... didn't reply to her messages. She told me how hurt she'd been and said she'd spent years wondering what she'd done that was so awful."

Nick's clearing took longer than some. Three months after he'd started the recipe he called.

"So, I've been making changes and nothing's happened."

"What do you mean by nothing?" I asked in my most innocent voice.

"I mean there's still no relationship."

"Tell me the nice things that have happened." I knew there must be some positive changes.

He thought.

"Well, actually things have happened. My ex- and I are getting on much better and she's letting me see more of the boys, in fact I've got them for most of the summer. That's progress."

He thought some more.

"Oh yes, I've joined a men's writing group. I've always wanted to write but just put it off and put it off. I'm starting to have fun with these guys."

"Anything else?"

"Yeah, there's one other thing. My mother's sister who lives in Italy wrote to me a few weeks ago. I haven't seen her since I was a little boy. Just out of the blue I get this letter and she's coming to visit me and the boys this summer."

"I'd say you're getting plenty of results. How far along are you with the changes?"

"I'd say about 60 percent," he replied

"Then you've got about 40 percent of the results still to come," I assured him before we said good-bye.

Nick is not alone in failing to recognize the positive changes that had happened in his life without a little gentle prodding. It's human nature to focus on the negative aspects of life, especially if we've gotten into the habit. Feng Shui serves to reorient us toward the Fortunate Blessings that the Universe has in store for all of us.

Chapter Fifteen

The Case of The Lemons
And Vinegar

*R*ichard's apartment was filled with color. Wonderful burgundies, deep rich greens, it was warm and cozy, the sort of place you step into and instantly feel comfortable. The floor plan and placement of furniture were harmonious, the artwork uplifting. Then I entered the kitchen, in the Relationship area.

Right there in the Relationship corner were the clues. In an immaculate kitchen, with nothing to clutter the white counter space, was a bowl of lemons, a bottle of Balsamic vinegar and a rack of sharp kitchen knives. Feng Shui is always straightforward, it doesn't pull any punches. It was apparent that his relationships had gone sour and involved both pain and separation. When I entered the bedroom this was confirmed. An almost dead ficus tree drooped by the window, incongruous in this well cared for apartment.

During our discussion it was no surprise when Richard confirmed the clues.

"My wife and I have been separated three months. We hate each other's guts. She phones me up screaming in the middle of the night and drags up all this stuff from the past about how I was never right for her. It's like she remembers the most minute little details of everything I ever said, like a criminal record or something. It's starting to affect my work."

Within a month of the changes, he called to tell me that he and his wife were on amiable terms. No, they weren't about to get back together, but they'd agreed to divorce and remain friends.

Are lemons, knives and vinegar always a sign of a painful relationship? By no means. Vinegar is a normal part of any kitchen's supplies. It was the placement, in this case, that was out of the ordinary. Lemons mixed with other fruits and placed in another area would not have indicated the same thing. Sometimes, to re-phrase Freud, a lemon is just a lemon!

Chapter Sixteen

The Case of The Igloo

*V*icky was an artist. Her tiny city apartment was colorful and whimsical, with plenty of healthy plants and three adorable Persian kittens. While there was lots of good energy, the moment I opened her bedroom closet I was sure the major difficulty was in Relationship. On the top shelf was a cardboard box. In black letters were the words Avoid Exposure To Extreme Heat or Cold. Beside it was another fairly large box marked IGLOO. Both boxes were in the area of Relationship. As usual, there were other clues, but the igloo was the key one.

"Vicky, let's play a game," I suggested during our consultation. "I'm going to say some words and you're going to finish the sentence. How about it?"

"Sure." Her face brightened.

"Marriage is an equal partnership that brings..."

"Pain, pain and more pain." The words sprang from her mouth before she had a chance to think.

Then she told me about her parents' marriage. Her father had been abusive to her mother and Vicky, an only child, felt powerless to do anything.

"How do you feel about relationships now?"

"I keep thinking maybe I'd like one but I'm afraid... I guess I haven't really seen a happy marriage and I'm not about to leap into the fire. Sure, I'm lonely but I figure I have lots of girlfriends and I'm better off this way. I have a good job as a graphic artist."

"What are your goals?"

"Well, I asked you in because in spite of everything I would like to have a relationship. I go out a lot with my friends but that's not the same as having a partner, is it?"

While there is always a central clue, there are usually many other minor pieces of evidence as well. Vicky's front door was partially blocked by an umbrella stand full of umbrellas. Placed in the Career/Life Journey, this indicated to me that she was constantly trying to protect herself from something bad that she feared was about to happen. She was ready for a rainy day, too ready. She confirmed this in her conversation.

"It's true, whenever things are going well, I sort of brace myself. You know, it looks good now but life's a roller coaster, the moment you're up, something happens to knock you down."

"Where do you think that belief came from?"

"I'm not sure."

"Let's try age eight."

I chose eight because by the front door I had noticed a collection of eight sharp stones, which appeared out of context. Let me hasten to add that sharp rocks are not always significant! It depends on the individual energy pattern, which is as precise as a fingerprint. Vicky's face suddenly lit up.

"I know what happened at age eight. I know exactly where I got this belief. My father went bankrupt just before my eighth birthday. Up until then we'd always lived comfortably and he'd opened up his own business. My mother was completely opposed to the idea and they argued all the time about it. When he did go bankrupt she screamed at him that he had ruined the family. I didn't understand exactly what had happened until I was about fourteen. We moved and I was yanked out of school. My father got a job working for someone else and he and my mother never got along after that. Once I screamed at them, "I wished you two would get a divorce. I left home as soon as I could get away."

"And yet you're still very close to your mother."

"How did you know?"

"Let's look in your Health area."

We walked over to the kitchen window where there was a table and lots of plants. By the side of the table hung a bird cage. Inside, instead of a live bird, sat two bright red and pink plush toys, obviously a mother bird with its baby.

"The placement of the toy birds in a cage would indicate ambivalence to the mother. While mother and child are connected and there is a softness, the relationship is one of imprisonment rather than empowerment. How does your mother feel about what you do... your art?"

"She's never thought much of it. She doesn't think I make enough money and nags me to get a "real" job. Then she writes me a cheque and calls me her baby. I've always felt sort of protective of her, she had a tough time when Dad's business went under."

"So to protect yourself in relationships you've built yourself an emotional igloo, right?"

"Absolutely."

Feng Shui is not conventional psychotherapy. However, by drawing a person's attention to what he or she has created, there is very often a shift in energy.

Sometimes, as a result of the unblocking, my clients will connect with an appropriate counselor or therapist. It's as though the Universe says, "Okay, you're unblocking. Here, I'll send you whatever and whomever you need to help you on your path!"

Over and over I've seen people's lives change so much that I'm prepared to offer a guarantee.

If my client follows the "Energy Recipe," fully as it's been given, there will be a steady process of clearing out and bringing in opportunity until at one year following the initial consultation, they will look back and say, "Wow, my life has improved!"

Which is not to say there won't be the usual daily challenges. The ups and downs go on forever; that's part of our life process. It makes me think of the Zen words, "Before Enlightenment, chop wood, carry water. After Enlightenment, chop wood, carry water."

Chapter Seventeen

Feng Shui Means Change: The Case of The Overstuffed House

By its very nature, Feng Shui welcomes change, sees it as an opportunity. Your decision to invite a Feng Shui consultant into your home is a decision to change. Once you have done the initial recipe, you have unblocked old patterns and laid the foundation for harmony. However, it's a constant process. We're forever moving things, rearranging, changing artwork, repainting walls and so on. Nothing in life is static.

Each week I walk through wherever I am living and do a check-up on the Chi flow and I usually find something! Just this week I did a walk through and discovered I'd carelessly blocked a doorway by placing a table with a broken leg behind it on its way to the dump. We hadn't quite gotten around to taking it to the car. I found clutter in my closet, two light bulbs which had burned out and a saw left in the yard. Each of these objects was weakening the energy and needed to be corrected before David and I noticed a depletion.

Think of Chi as a supply of energy. When batteries run down you replace them, when your light bulbs burn out, you do the same thing. Once you begin to notice the energy of the objects you live with you begin to form the habit of awareness.

Weakened Chi begins like a blocked sink. A few hairs, a particle of food and the sink still drains but then one day it's blocked and you can't get it unblocked. Gray water backs up and you have to call a plumber. In the following case we'll take a look at an extreme case of "blocked Chi."

I'll never forget the New England house I was called into by Boris, a wonderfully witty writer. The moment I stepped in the front door I knew exactly what health problem to expect. Every possible flat surface was piled with papers, books, and "stuff." Cans filled with tools, telephones wrapped in their own cords, dusty typewriters. Even the bed was partially covered with newspapers. The kitchen stove had clearly not been used for some time, it was heaped with cans of food and dog dishes. And what about the saddle on the maple chopping block? Did he ride his horse while chopping onions?

I thought to myself, this man is wasting his money on a consultation, he'll never be able to clear this out, it would take a lifetime. His daughter, my client, had either blackmailed or charmed him into phoning me. I dreaded giving him my assessment.

There was so much junk in the house I couldn't even focus on a central clue. Then suddenly, as I carefully maneuvered myself through the bathroom in Health and Family, I glanced at a pile of papers. On top was the headline which announced the sinking of the *Titanic*. Aha! Not only was it an excellent clue, that paper with its historic headline must be worth something. At the end of my reading I finished by saying, "The placement of the newspaper article on the *Titanic* would indicate that there is a potentially serious health problem and probably some difficulty with family members. I would suggest a possible high blood pressure." The congestion in the house hinted at similar constrictions in the body, something that might cause high blood pressure.

My client had been staring at me throughout the reading in a rather unnerving way. He looked, to put it mildly, cynical. Perhaps I was reading this one incorrectly. Okay, remember your original promise? The day it doesn't work, you go back to your writing and forget being a Feng Shui practitioner. It was years since I'd abandoned my novel. Good thing I'd called it *Making Mother Immortal!*

Then he began to talk very quickly. "I'm being treated for high blood pressure and my family's driving me nuts. This is my parents' house, most of the stuff here belonged to them. They left the house to me with the understanding I could live here as long as I wanted. When I die or if I sell, the money from the sale is to be divided among my brothers. I have two, one's a dentist, the other's a lawyer. I've always been the black sheep, the one who couldn't really make it on his own, the nutty writer, so my parents felt sorry for me, especially after my wife walked out with the kids. They left me the house. My brothers make six figure salaries. But they're pressuring me all the time to sell the house and move somewhere smaller. I get it from their wives too. No wonder I have high blood pressure! Who wouldn't?" He glared at me. "So, what do you recommend?"

"How would you feel about clearing out some of the stuff?"

"Where would I begin? Just thinking about it makes my blood pressure shoot up."

Though I saw his point, I suggested he begin by relocating the paper with the *Titanic* headline, perhaps by donating it to the local museum. He finally agreed. He also thought he could get someone in to help him clear the bathroom, the Health area, and the small study upstairs, also in the Health area.

"I could see if I can find time for that, but this isn't going to happen overnight."

"That's fine, you do it when you feel like it and I'll go through some changes you can take as long as you like with. It's better to go slowly here."

Let me reiterate: the speed at which changes are made is important. If they're made too quickly chances are you'll actually get sick. Indeed after my experience with one client, I'm super-careful in cautioning to go slowly, only one change every twenty four hours, sometimes longer.

I'll never forget Sherry. The recipe for her and her husband contained fourteen steps which I suggested be done over a twenty seven-day period. Each step was fairly small and easy, but there was an energy pattern of poor health which indicated that it was extremely important to proceed methodically. She agreed. Two days later she called sounding terrible.

"I've come down with a fever and everything's blocked. I feel awful."

"What changes have you made?"

"Well, after you left, my husband had to go on a business trip and I figured I'd just do the changes right away. I guess that wasn't such a great idea?"

No it wasn't and it's something that happens from time to time no matter how much I caution clients to go slow. As I mentioned earlier, we dubbed it the Feng Shui Flu.

To return to Boris, my writer-client, I was not too optimistic especially when I didn't hear from him for a month. Finally, I decided to give him a call and ask how the cures were coming.

"Haven't gotten around to it yet," he said. "I'll call you."

Six months went by before I heard from him again.

"I've cleaned out the rooms you said affected my health," he began. "And though I find it hard to believe, the doctor tells me my blood pressure's down and he's taken me off medication. I'm thinking maybe I'll have someone in to take the whole damn mess away."

A year later he called again. This time he was euphoric. "I'm a new man. Never felt better. I had the whole place cleaned out, couldn't do it myself. I've decided to sell the house and move somewhere smaller. I'm leaving for Italy next week, figured it was time to take a break and let my brothers take care of things for a change!"

Shortly after he returned from Europe, Boris sold the house and moved into a smaller one. The next time I heard from him it was to tell me he was getting married. He went on: "I'd say my life has changed a whole lot since the Feng Shui. That house never did feel right, I should've sold it as soon as my parents died."

How Creative Is Your Clutter?

Most of my clients have cleaned and tidied the house before I arrive, so much so that when I return home, I feel obliged to get out my own vacuum cleaner. While cleanliness and tidiness generally do improve energy, there's no need to be obsessive. In fact some people need a certain degree of clutter to be creative; this is the energy of the artist.

My dear friend Madeleine Partous, the extraordinary woman who midwifed my novels, looked defiant when I entered her office one day.

"I know, I know, I can't see over my papers, but don't tell me to get rid of them. I need them. I can't think creatively if everything's sterile."

She's right. Her energy thrives on doing many things at once. Sometimes, like the whirling dervish, performing movements that would make most of us collapse from dizziness, there are energy patterns that thrive on swimming upstream.

Madeleine did however agree to unblock the back of her kitchen and relocate her laundry. Six months later she entered a wonderful relationship. Formerly a person who lived alone, ate out and rarely spent an evening at home, she now enjoys eating in, has adopted two dogs and freely admits to being happier than she's been in her life! 🐾

Chapter Eighteen

The Case of The Anemic House

*F*lorence's house looked like something out of *Architectural Digest*. It was the antithesis of Boris's house — remember the witty writer? Not a piece of clutter in any of the rooms. Cream wall-to-wall, textured cream furniture impeccably placed, white blinds to protect against the extreme heat of this southern town.

The kitchen was also white, there was a vase of white lilies on the table and in the entrance stood a beautiful white marble fountain.

It was apparent that Florence's house had an excess of the metal element, represented by creams, whites and pale colors, stone, and, of course, metal.

From the start, I felt that the owner, like the house, would probably suffer from anemia.

That proved correct. Florence was currently under medical treatment for pernicious anemia.

She was eager to do whatever would help but because she loved her all-white house, it was not a simple matter of bringing in accents of reds or pinks, the colors of fire, which balances an excess of metal. We had to be more subtle.

"How do you feel about candles?" I asked when we'd discussed findings.

"I love candles."

She agreed instantly to place large cream colored candles in each room, as well as a photograph of the pyramids, which, even in a black and white photograph, with their triangular shape, represent the fire element. Her one concession to the color red was in the kitchen, where she agreed to place a big blue pottery bowl of red apples.

"I like apples, that's not a problem," she smiled. "Tell me, I've been thinking of getting a dog. What do you think?"

I looked around at the immaculate expanses of creamy wall-to-wall carpet. As the owner of a cat, a Pekinese, an English bulldog, two Russian wolfhounds, and a Vietnamese pot-bellied pig, I could imagine how the house would look after one rainy day. Sometimes I must confess I fantasize about an all-white house!

"Do you mean a dog or a puppy?"

"A puppy."

"How much time do you spend at home?"

"Actually I'm here a lot. I work in the darkroom in the mornings and I'm usually at my desk the rest of the time."

"A puppy, like all animals, represents the fire element," I told her. "That would certainly help melt down the metal."

Florence made the changes within a month. Several months later she called to tell me about her puppy.

"He's the sweetest puppy. I got him from the animal shelter. He's part retriever, part lab and he's as good as gold. We're having a great time."

"How are you feeling?"

"Well, you wouldn't believe this but my hemoglobin's come way up and I have more energy than I've had since I bought this place. You must come by and meet my Ben. That's what I've named the pup," she added before I had a chance to ask.

Chapter Nineteen

The Case of The Poison Arrows

*M*y parents are in their eighties. My father caught malaria when he served in New Guinea during World War II, the Australian Air Force, which created a chain of health problems involving the pancreas and liver. In spite of this, all his life he has played competitive tennis. My mother has what my father refers to as a "Rolls Royce engine." She enjoyed wonderful health and also played competition tennis until her early eighties. Then all that seemed to change.

They sold their beach house on a tropical island and bought a townhouse in a nearby retirement village. As mother said, "The village provides all levels of care and if we ever needed help we're provided for." They moved in and continued with tennis and walks on the beach.

Mother, who had mild arthritis which had never required medication or treatment, was now in constant pain. And six weeks before a scheduled visit to America to visit my brother and me, my father, while serving on the tennis court, was overcome with dizziness. A few days later, when he got into the car, he felt dizzy once more and slumped forward onto the steering wheel. His doctor admitted him to hospital for testing and diagnosed him as having some degree of congestive heart failure. Sadly they canceled their trip to Hawaii and America. My father was released from hospital and prescribed a barrage of medications.

Then the real nightmare began. He developed stomach pains so severe that he was unable to sleep. His doctor referred him to a specialist. Neither could come up with a solution. Finally, poring through the pages of medical textbooks, my father decided that the pain was the result of a medication he was taking for his heart. He cut down the dose and the pain receded, but he felt exhausted. Meanwhile my mother was having dizzy spells and her arthritic pain was so bad she could scarcely walk.

When David and I and my brother, Arthur, who lives in California, flew into Brisbane, we were surprised to be met by our parents who, in spite of poor health had driven in forty miles to meet us. They looked frail but we had a wonderful reunion.

That night, on a breezy balcony overlooking the ocean, we caught up. Now I must mention that my parents' reaction when I told them I was a Feng Shui practitioner was less than gratifying. "Fung what, darling?" They neither understood it nor took it seriously.

However, over the next few weeks, as I explained what I do, they became more receptive. Finally, I asked their permission to check their house. They agreed.

"After all it can't do any harm, I suppose," was their attitude.

The moment I had permission I was thrilled, because, though I don't "do" Feng Shui unless I am asked, I couldn't help noticing my parents' "clues."

Naturally I was particularly concerned with areas which affected and reflected their health, so I was both alarmed and delighted when I made my discoveries. Alarmed because of how potent the affect on their health had been, delighted because I could see how to remove the blocks.

In the garage I unearthed a machete. In the living room, I found the collection of bow and poison arrows given my father by the natives of New Guinea during the war. In another health area I discovered his Japanese bayonet, the one he used to trim the privet hedges when old Mrs. Richard-next-door back in Melbourne complained the white flowers made her sneeze. There were other minor clues, easy to remedy, such as the placement of the bed. With their permission, I relocated the machete and arrows and moved several pieces of furniture. They were relieved to find that nothing drastic was required.

We had our best visit ever, took a ferry cruise around the island through what is now a World Heritage site with a large nesting area for birds migrating from the north and one of the world's largest dugong feeding areas. We picnicked, admired the birds which eat from my mother's hands, took beach walks and sat for long talks every night after dinner on the balcony of a wonderful seaside restaurant. The day of our departure was so sad. At the airport we wished they were healthy enough to make the trip. We promised to return soon.

In the next few weeks the changes were dramatic. My father's energy level improved daily. And over the next six weeks my mother's aches and pains virtually disappeared. My mother now reads everything on Feng Shui she can get her hands on! ❧

Chapter Twenty

Hartmann Lines: The Case of The Sickly House

*W*hen I first began to practice Feng Shui I was puzzled by a pattern which often occurred in houses and offices. Several clues were arranged along definite lines, almost as though a grid had been drawn running through the various rooms of the building, cutting through each floor. Along these lines I'd find all sorts of evidence that the energy was depleted; objects would be broken or neglected, there was clutter and disturbing artwork; sometimes a dripping tap, a leak in the ceiling, light bulbs burned out, clocks which had stopped. I'd have my client correct these as part of the Recipe, but I needed to know more about these mysterious "lines."

I could find nothing in the Feng Shui books. Then one morning in Sedona I was invited to a workshop on Earth Healing given by Christan Hummel. Christan described a system of working with the Nature Spirits, called Devas, and the land itself to clear pollution. During the workshop I learned about Geopathic Stress and grid lines. My experiences with the lines began to make sense.

I redoubled my efforts to search the literature for information and then one day my friend Barbara Bronfman sent me a printout she'd found on the Internet — finally, here was what I needed.

In the early 1930s, French dowsing expert, Abbe Merme, wrote that the radiations associated with underground veins of water were "transmitted from floor to floor in any house situated above them. One might be exposed to them in a workshop, a factory, an office as well as in the flat on the tenth floor of a building. It is in a bedroom that their presence is the most harmful, for in such a case, the affected individual is not only subjected to the bad effects of such radiations but is also deprived of sound and regenerative sleep. Impaired health results in consequence, and the affected person suffers from various ailments which neither he nor the doctor can account for."

Before the first World War, in his book, *Dowsing*, W. M. Trinder wrote: "There seems to be very little doubt that rays given off by subterranean water are, if continuous contact is maintained with them, definitely harmful to both human beings and plants. I have known instances of people suffering from nerves and also from rheumatism. In these cases the sufferers were spending a large part of every twenty four hours right over a subterranean stream and this was slowly having the most deleterious effect on their health."

In addition to Geopathic Zones of Disturbance, the information Barbara sent me also described a Hartmann Net, an invisible grid system that covers the earth's surface. This was discovered by and named after the German medical doctor, Ernst Hartmann.

The lines of the Hartmann Net run north to south and east to west and the radiation emitted by these lines, especially at points of intersection, can, according to Dr. Hartmann, harm persons who spend extended periods of time above them, so it is crucial that frequently used furniture such as beds, desk and chairs, not be placed directly over them.

Most of us are aware, more or less, of the potential harm of over-exposure to electro-magnetic fields, such as those emitted by power lines and even by computers and household items such as clock radios. Less is known however about the potential harm of geomagnetic fields, referred also to as "earth radiation." The literature explained why my "clues" frequently occurred in a pattern. It was clear they occurred along lines of potentially harmful energy like those described by Dr. Hartmann. I found I could locate the lines by using simple metal dowsing rods and began to demonstrate my findings to clients, recommending that furniture such as beds, chairs and sofas be relocated.

Shortly afterwards I was invited to Feng Shui an apartment in the southwest. After I'd located a Hartmann Line which ran horizontally right through the pillows of the master bed, I asked the young couple: "Have either of you had increasing headaches, sinus problems, allergies, sore throats, neck pains or nightmares?"

They looked at each other and began to laugh. The young man burst out, "Are you kidding? Guess where I'm going right after you finish? I have an appointment with an allergist. Every time I get into bed the sinusitis starts and I've also had this pain in my neck."

His wife cut in, "And I've had nightmares ever since we moved in three months ago. I can't figure it out, we've never had this before we moved here."

Fortunately we were able to move the bed out from the wall. Within two weeks all the symptoms disappeared. Sometimes however, I find illness which has been developing for years. Clearly in a long-term case a return to good health can't be achieved instantly.

While all sorts of health problems have responded well to treatment of the Hartmann Lines, the most common response from newborn babies through to people in their eighties has been improved sleep.

Short of calling in a dowsing expert, what can you do yourself if you suspect you may be sleeping or working on a Hartmann Line? The North American Dowsers suggest the following:

1. Since metal will amplify the radiation, consider replacing your mattress and bedsprings with either an all-cotton futon on a wooden frame, or a mattress and "foundation" which uses foam rubber and other materials for support, instead of metal. Please keep in mind that all mattresses contain flame-retardants, and many will also contain formaldehyde, both of which are highly toxic chemicals.

2. If the Geopathic Zone of Disturbance is a relatively narrow one, a bed, desk or chair can be relocated to a neutral area. If on the other hand, the radiation is emitted by a number of overlapping underground veins of water or earthquake faults, or even one very wide "river," treating an all-pervasive field of radiation affecting a large area of your home, there are "interrupters" available. When properly placed by an experienced dowser, these will literally push the radiation back into the earth.

Currently there is work being done to perfect "harmonizers" to reverse the polarity of the electromagnetic field from negative to positive. While available in some places in Europe, Germany and Switzerland to mention two countries, these are not, to my knowledge common yet in North America. Clearly, this is a field which needs more research as well as public awareness.

Chapter Twenty One

The Case of The Lightning Strike

The moment I entered the living room of Sarah and Alex's house, even before I unwrapped the metal rods from my briefcase, I could sense the Hartmann. The line of intense energy ran right through the center of the living room, bisected the dining room and exited through the garden. This particular line felt more intense than most of the ones I identify.

I stood in front of a large painting. It felt powerful, very yang and featured a red figure who appeared to me to be shouting, against an arid, sunburned background. The Hartmann line ran straight through what I dubbed the "Red Man." I examined the corresponding wall in the dining room. Another painting, another strong yang image. More reds and oranges. Each of the images was dominated by the element Fire, represented by the reds and oranges.

As I explained this to the couple, they couldn't contain themselves.

"That's exactly where the lightning struck!" burst out Sarah.

We sat down and they told me about the fire which had destroyed a large section of their house just months ago.

"I was home with the kids," Sarah told me. "It looked like a storm was building outside but we often get these really big storms here, so I didn't think much about it. Then there was a big bang and I smelled smoke. It was coming from the roof! I called 911 and bundled the kids into the car. By the time the firemen arrived the house was on fire. You know where the lightning had struck? You've got it, right down what you're calling the Hartmann Line."

We worked with placement and balanced the elements, adding the Water element to balance Fire and introducing changes to boost the Water. They say lightning only strikes the same place once, but the couple didn't want to take any chances! ᴥ

Chapter Twenty Two

Our Money, Ourselves:
The Case of The Secret Closet

*W*e all want prosperity, and let's face it, when we say the word, most of us are thinking of money. The area of Number Four in the Bagua, sometimes referred to as "wealth" or "prosperity" is the area of wind. Wind represents the movement of energy, the source.

I like the term Fortunate Blessings for this area as it brings to mind good fortune in all areas of our lives, and when it comes down to it, we desire money to bring us good feelings, happiness.

When we're in harmonious relationship with ourselves and others, chances are we'll be in vibrant good health, enjoy our creativity and in turn, receive recognition for our unique contributions. If we focus solely on money without overall harmony, however, chances are we'll short-change ourselves.

I recall a woman who phoned early in my practice.

"My husband and I would like you to come and look at our Wealth area," she began. "We don't need you to do the whole house."

Before she could tell me the details I explained the way I practice. "I could do that, but I'm afraid you'd be wasting your money. To figure out what's happening with your wealth, I need to look at everything else inside and outside your house. Sure, I could make suggestions to enhance one area, and you'd probably see improvement right away, but it would be a quick fix. Somewhere down the line you'd be back to square one. I don't consider that Feng Shui. If we make adjustments to every area that needs it you can build the foundation that produces wealth." They decided to go ahead.

As it turned out, though the energy in Fortunate Blessings was low, it was the result of a complex pattern. I knew that this couple had the ability to generate all the money they wanted. Structurally the prosperity area was strong and outside there was a beautiful red bougainvillea climbing on a red brick wall. The property was protected by mountain ranges which in the classical Form School of Feng Shui represented dragon, tortoise and tiger, with a phoenix in front; a perfect configuration.

The problem lay in the basement. In a small storage room I sensed an unusual pattern of energy. In one corner was a stack of old paintings, the gold frames dusty. Carefully I examined each. Sure enough, there was the clue. It was a reproduction of a work by the Spanish painter, Goya, of a military execution. The paintings were blocking a heavy armoire. When I opened the doors I discovered a collection of what appeared to be antique guns. Aha!

But that wasn't all. Something about the armoire wasn't quite right. It was dim in the room, lit by a single 40-watt light bulb. I checked the area around the armoire. There was a horizontal piece of wood showing on the wall above the top of the armoire. Cautiously I pushed the armoire, not wanting to trigger an antique gun — definitely bad Feng Shui for the practitioner to shoot herself!

I decided not only was the armoire heavy but that if I were to explore behind it I needed the owners' permission.

I explained about the armoire and suggested we move it.

"No problem," said the man. "We haven't been down there for years."

Sure enough, behind the heavy piece of furniture was a cobwebby door. When he turned the handle it opened a little way, then stopped. He forced his way in, then returned to forage for a flashlight. Finally the three of us stood in the doorway.

I half expected to find a corpse, it was the perfect set-up. But instead, the small room was piled high with old newspapers and empty wine bottles. The newspapers were yellow with age, with that characteristic moldy smell.

Have you looked at a newspaper in the last twenty four hours? News is practically synonymous with bad news. Just think how many murders, acts of brutality, terrorism and petty crime are recorded in a four-foot-high pile of papers! And what about the wine bottles? Wine is associated with the good things of life, celebration, feasting. But empty wine bottles? The good things of life are drained. Memories.

I resumed my snoop and creep while the couple went back to the living room. As I completed my search I came up with other minor clues. I have never yet found a clue which was not part of a network of small evidences.

My conclusion? It was clear that my clients' beliefs about money were associated with fear of lack; the gun collection (guns are used to defend); the hidden door, the bad news contained in the old papers and empty bottles. Coming from such a belief of lack, it would not matter how much money we bring in, it would constantly flow away leaving us with a shortage of fortunate blessings.

After working with my clients on their beliefs about money, I left them with a customized recipe.

Then I waited for their report. Six weeks later they called.

"I don't know whether it's the Feng Shui or not," the woman began, "but you wouldn't believe what's happened. We never told you this but my husband was having trouble with a partner who was trying to get him out and take over the company. We were in the middle of a legal battle. That's why we called you. Well, it's all been solved and we've landed our biggest contract in three years."

Chapter Twenty Three

Why the Rich Get Richer: The Case of The Naked Backs

I'm frequently invited to Feng Shui beautiful houses which clearly belong to the rich. While there may be all sorts of energetic constrictions, repeatedly I notice that by and large, the Number Four areas are well-kept and decorated. One of the most attractive areas I've seen is a beautiful patio shaded by large maple trees. From the branches hang dozens of birdfeeders which are filled regularly. The material wealth of this family comes as no surprise. Chances are the richer you are, the more likely you are to have other people who help you run your life smoothly. It becomes a cycle. More money, more help, everything well-cared for and running efficiently.

If, however, money were the only ingredient in our Fortunate Blessings, I wouldn't find clues in these well-tended Number Four areas which indicate that all may not be flowing as smoothly as the money.

It was apparent from the moment I parked my car that my clients had all the material wealth you could wish for. The house rose majestically in front of me from gardens filled with spring flowers: daffodils, tulips, irises. A gardener knelt in the soft earth, weeding.

As usual I began my Feng Shui with an inspection of the property. Everything seemed cared for, not a single clue. The swimming pool was perfectly maintained. So was the tennis court and every square inch of the garden. Yet, as I examined the Number Four area of the house, I found my first clue. The area included a small cinema with red velvet seats. But at the back of the room was a glass cabinet filled with shells.

I'm very fond of shells. Some of the happiest times of my childhood were spent on a small island in Port Philip Bay, south of Melbourne, shell hunting with my mother. The shells we both valued most were the cowries, the ones with the polished backs and tiny teeth. Shells are lovely objects. But the placement of this large collection struck me as odd.

I moved into the living room and examined the area of relationship. Sure enough I found my second clue; a painting of a nude woman's head, shoulders and back. The back appeared vulnerable. As I moved through the house I found several similar paintings: nude female backs.

By the time I'd completed my inspection, it was clear that while there was enormous wealth, it did not bring the joyful relationships you'd hope for.

After we'd completed the walk-through of the property and house, my client, Clara, and I sat in the garden. I explained my findings and concluded.

"In the area of relationships there is considerable loyalty and affection, but there's nothing happening right now. There is a fear of being taken advantage of, of being used because of money, and this creates difficulty in finding any permanent relationship."

Clara confirmed this. "I've been married three times," she told me, and each time I feel I've been taken advantage of. I'm afraid to get into another relationship in case the same thing happens. I do have a lot of wonderful friends, so it's not all that bad, but I get lonely."

I suggested she begin by looking carefully at the nude backs. The final step in her recipe was to relocate the shells. The placement of the shell collection in her cinema was a reminder of the past, memories of relationships no longer animated. After all, no matter how beautiful a shell, it is something left behind that was once inhabited by a living creature.

When last Clara and I spoke, she was bubbling with new energy. "My attitude seems to have changed. I have more energy and I'm involved with all sorts of exciting things. I still don't have a romance, but I don't feel that same kind of loneliness I told you about when you came, remember?"

Chapter Twenty Four

The Case of The Vinegar and Bleach

Remember the case of the lemons, Balsamic vinegar and knives? In that case, their placement indicated difficulty in relationship. Shortly afterwards I was called into a famous New Mexican restaurant, a favorite watering hole of celebrities which in the 1950s included the late Grace Kelly before she became Princess Grace of Monaco.

The restaurant, renowned as much for its ambience as its food, appeared to be inexplicably slowing down. I discovered the clue in the wine cellar. Along with wonderful wines, on a bottom shelf was a large bottle of vinegar and some Chlorox bleach. Neither item belonged on this shelf. It was apparent, because of their placement in Fortunate Blessings, that profits had turned sour, literally being bleached. This was confirmed by some blocked doors, placement of a dumpster and position of desks with their backs to the door. Once the corrections were made the restaurant began to reclaim its longtime prosperity. 🐛

Chapter Twenty Five

The Case of The
One-Winged Owl

I knew Bernice was having problems with prosperity the moment I stepped onto the porch. Leaning against the wall was a ship's anchor. Now a ship's anchor is a fine thing — for a ship. But something about it seemed just too weighed down for the energy of this particular property. By the door was an attractive Mexican pot filled with four cigarette butts. The entrance door led into a narrow hallway to the kitchen and on this particular morning a pile of clothes, obviously due for the laundry, was piled beside a freezer. The back of the house commanded a lovely view from its pretty patio, but the big sun umbrella was faded, the white canvas torn.

As I moved from room to room the big picture began to assemble in my mind. I stood on the elegant terrace with a finely sculptured bird nicely set in a corner. The sunlit hills ahead of me were serene and beautiful. I was about to return to the kitchen when suddenly I turned back and stopped to examine the bird sculpture more closely.

What sort of bird was it? It was large and made from stone. Then I realized what disturbed me. Though slightly abstract, it was not abstract enough to miss the central fact. There was one wing, folded into its side. The bird looked something like an owl. But where was the other wing? By the time I returned to the kitchen I knew how we could rearrange the energies.

"The placement of the anchor indicates that an aspect of career is being pulled down, handicapped," I told Bernice as we sat at her kitchen table. "There is a feeling of burnout, of working too hard for too little. Part of this is connected to taking care of someone else's dirty laundry. And the placement of the one-winged owl confirms that though money comes in, it's as though it drains away and can't really fly the way it should." Bernice laughed wryly.

"That pretty well says it. I own a hot air balloon company that's doing well, but as soon as the money comes in we seem to always have unexpected expenses and it goes just as fast as it comes in. I'm tired of working with not much to show for it. And what you said about someone else's laundry. I take care of my mother and she's always telling me I'm doing the wrong thing."

Normally I give a careful recipe and my client proceeds with the steps in order. This time, however, Bernice was adamant. "Let's get this bird out right now!" She headed out the door to the owl. "Here, give me a hand."

I eyed the bird dubiously. It looked very heavy and I was not eager to put my back out. But she was already heaving at it. I gripped the other side. "Where do you want it?"

"We're taking it straight to the dumpster."

The sculpture was obviously worth something, but when it came down to it I wouldn't wish a one-winged owl on anyone, especially someone in the flying business! Together we heaved it into the dumpster and it landed on top of some garbage bags with a resounding thunk.

"I never liked that bird anyway," Bernice told me as we returned to the kitchen. "Now, what about the anchor?"

Shortly afterwards her company began to fly high once more. 🐾

Chapter Twenty Six

Creating a Strong Core: The Case of The Crooked House

*F*ive is the number associated in the Bagua with the Tai Chi, or neutral center, the core. Ideally this is the part of our dwelling which is strong, serene and well-grounded.

Morrie's house was surrounded by beautifully landscaped grounds. The house was L shaped, but the potentially weak area, the part which was outside the floor plan, had been strengthened by the addition of a wooden fence with a locked gate. The street outside was busy but the moment I stepped through the gate it was almost like a monastery garden; the sound of water, birds and everywhere, well-tended flowers.

Inside, the house was clean and orderly. Still, something felt out of the ordinary. Because of the L shape, the front door was situated in the Number Five, the Tai Chi, which meant a mixed bag. The entrance as a core, which is also the point of arrivals and departures can, unless we are very mindful, easily produce stress. It's a pattern I've found frequently among people such as flight attendants whose careers take them away from home on a regular basis. Even though this entrance was filled with healthy plants, it still felt wrong.

The area projected slightly and the door had been set on an angle. I felt off-balance. The placement of furniture made it clear that Morrie felt somehow helpless. And though in this well-ordered house it seemed improbable, the word "suicide" popped into my mind.

Now this has only happened once before. It was a similar house design. The Tai Chi was unbalanced and my client told me that she had never felt at home in the world and had actually attempted suicide several times.

When I gave Morrie my reading I said, "There is much which is beautiful and harmonious in this pattern. Money is not a problem, you generate all the money you need. You've achieved a great deal of success with career and have good friends whom you help and who help you. But there is a sense of feeling not quite as though you belong, of literally being off-balance." I paused. He was staring straight into my eyes. "There is almost a sense of not wanting to go on at some level."

Morrie actually turned pale.

"I'm getting shivers," he said. "I've always felt the way you describe, ever since I was a little boy. I've actually considered suicide. I have a great respect for life and would never do it, but I've always felt somehow like I don't belong here. I wonder what it's like on the other side. Once I actually called a suicide hotline. Right now I have wonderful friends and that helps a lot." He paused to think. "It's like I say to myself, what am I supposed to be doing here?"

This was the first time I actually recommended a major architectural change. The door had to be set straight. Morrie didn't bat an eyelid.

"I have a friend who's an architect. We can do it right away."

Fortunately money was not an issue. They reset the door and Morrie later called.

"I can't believe the difference it makes. Every time I come in I feel safe. I never felt unsafe before," he laughed. "But now I feel safe. Does that make sense to you? But something's been bothering me. Did I choose a house with a crooked door because I felt uncentered, or did I just happen to move in here and because I had tendencies, they became worse here?"

As we discussed earlier, I believe that we tend to select living spaces which resonate with our energy patterns. As these shift, we either redecorate, remodel or move.

Each of us has "issues." For example, if we have money issues, we may choose a house with a weak area of Fortunate Blessings and/or a weak area of Service. If we're working on an unhappy childhood, this will similarly be reflected. Does this sound way off-target? I see it over and over. Just yesterday a client called to ask me to look at her new house.

Six months ago we worked together on her first Feng Shui consultation. That initial session revealed that there were health problems relating to childhood and her relationship with her mother. After completing the recipe, her health problem, a series of allergies, cleared right up and she felt more energetic.

Her new house was strong in the areas the previous one had been weak, indicating that she had moved old energetic blocks. However there were a few small indications that there was still a vestige of handicap from her childhood relationship with her mother. These were fairly straightforward to deal with. By the time she completes her move, she'll have laid a solid foundation to enjoy her creativity and begin to have fun.

Let's return to the Number Five. The Tai Chi is an area which ideally does not contain staircases, too many doors or windows. Artwork in this area should reflect serenity and strength, the sort of thing we like to have as our center of unity.

Chapter Twenty Seven

The Case of The Bullfights

The moment I set foot in Brian's house he confronted me, arms folded across his chest.

"I have to tell you I don't really believe in Feng Shui."

While this is not my favorite greeting, it happens quite frequently. The words still, for many people, conjure up all sorts of witchcraft and skullduggery!

Brian continued. "Like I told you on the phone, my friend Claude says you helped him. I figured the worst that can happen is I've wasted my money."

Brian's Tai Chi area was painted a rich bright blue, a color in Feng Shui which represents the wood element. Hanging from the walls were a set of black-framed prints of Spanish bullfights; the matadors with their brilliant pink-lined capes, the picadors with the sharp weapons used to goad the bull; the charging bull, his side streaming blood. The theme of the Tai Chi was continued in the bedroom, only this time it was a collection of hunting prints complete with a stuffed and mounted stag's head. In the living room, in front of a marble fireplace lay a bearskin rug.

Brian accompanied me as we walked through each room. As usual I pointed out the areas in which the energy was high, as well as those which I felt could be enhanced.

At the end of my reading, I concluded, "While there is an understanding of money and considerable ability to deal with every aspect of material wealth, relationships tend to be adversarial. It's as though you get in your own way. You attract the good things of life, including relationships, then it's as though you deliberately set out to destroy them. This appears to originate right at your center. It's as though you've had to fight to survive and fighting has become habit for you."

I half expected Brian to throw me out. Finally he unfolded his arms.

"I'm not an easy person to live with," he began. "I've been married three times. Does that shock you?"

I shook my head. "I guess I'd like to know what your goals are and what you want to achieve from Feng Shui."

"I figure you could maybe tell me how to keep a relationship."

"I can't do that, but I can help you bring more harmony into your house. How would you feel about following some suggestions?"

"You tell me what they are and I'll tell you how I'd feel."

"How would you feel about relocating the bullfighting prints? And painting the foyer? The blue walls are literally snuffing out the energy." This was correct. The Tai Chi is in the element Earth, which is controlled by Wood. Earth is produced from Fire. The spilled blood of the bulls and the hot pink of the capes certainly represented fire, but their violent energy was creating on-going stress at Brian's core. I knew from other clues that there had been difficulty in childhood.

"In other words you're telling me to change my house."

"I'm not telling you to do anything. I'm simply suggesting changes that will help the harmony of this house."

He stood up. "I'll get back to you."

Six weeks later Brian called. He sounded defensive. "I moved the bull-fighters and painted the walls that dirty yellow color you suggested."

"How do you feel?"

"To tell you the truth it doesn't feel as bad as I thought it would. You'll be pleased with me though. I sold the bullfighting prints."

I remained silent, amazed at the change. As he talked, his voice was becoming softer, friendlier.

"And I bought a huge photo of a spectacular sunrise over the Pacific."

I knew Brian was going to be okay. He called regularly every week or so. One day he told me he'd given away the hunting prints and the bearskin rug. "I'm taking flying lessons," he added.

"How do you feel?"

"Terrific."

Brian never did tell me any details of his childhood. I didn't need to know. The last time we spoke he was flying a small plane regularly. He sounded happier than I'd ever heard him. I knew that the corrections to his center of unity, the Tai Chi had triggered a whole series of energetic shifts which would create confidence and eventually joy.

Recently a friend of Brian's called. "Brian said I have to have you Feng Shui my house."

"How is Brian?"

"Good. Real good. We're having a relationship. He's a great guy."

Chapter Twenty Eight

Exchanging Service: The Case of The Leaking Garage

*T*he area of Number Six is also referred to as Helpful People and Helpful Friends. These are accurate descriptions but I prefer Service as it implies not simply receiving but giving, an equal exchange of service. It represents the going out of our energies, of somehow making the world a little better and in return, being receptive to the Fortunate Blessings from those around us.

When David and I bought the Colonel's cottage we knew it had problems. Built in 1900, it had originally been a summer house. The Colonel had lived most of the year down by the St. Lawrence River in the area now known as "Old Montreal," a charming area of cobble-stoned streets, a seaman's church, fine cathedral and old warehouses now converted to artists' lofts and upscale boutiques, together with an out-door marketplace.

The voyage up the "mountain" had taken half a day by horse and buggy. Once there, the Colonel and his family settled into the stucco cottage with its wide verandahs commanding a view of apple orchards and below, the then small city with the ships in the harbor.

As I mentioned earlier, we bought it because it was love at first sight, our only criterion for buying a property. It did, however, as the agent pointed out, lack "curb appeal." The front lawn grew decaying tricycles and soggy stuffed animals.

The first year we replaced the rickety wooden steps which climbed steeply up the mountainside, with wide stone steps winding gently between English perennials. We opened up the dark hallway with French doors and built a wooden deck and a lion's head fountain.

In the next few years we painted the entire house, cleared out old wallpaper and carpeting, and as I described earlier, replaced the rotting deck of Illumination outside the kitchen. Our careers were flourishing, our daughter living a rich and happy life pursuing her artistic goals, our animals much loved and exuberant. We were very happy.

Then irritating glitches surfaced. The flow of money slowed to a trickle. We couldn't understand it until one spring morning we discovered that part of the garage ceiling had caved in. The problem was apparent. The house, set into the "belly of the dragon" has stone terraces on each of its three floors, each with city views and some with views of a piece of woodland on the other side of an old stone wall. Water was somehow leaking from a terrace down into the floor below.

We called in a contractor who groaned and basically told us we'd have to remortgage the house to take up the stone, locate the leak and then rebuild part of the garage. The problem was that because of the leak, the flow of money had slowed. We were faced with a problem which confronts many of my clients. How do you generate money when you don't have the funds to take the necessary steps?

Finally we found a contractor who agreed to do the work. The problem was, we thought, solved.

Not so. Money, though slightly improved, was not back to normal. That winter brought the terrible Montreal ice storm which paralyzed the city for three weeks. Our street, one of the steepest in the city, was strewn with fallen power lines, piles of branches. It was impassable. The Canadian Army actually set up base in the road at the foot of our steps.

In spite of our difficulties, the house was extremely blessed. No major trees came down, just some branches. But as soon as the ice thawed, we noticed that the ceiling in the foyer was leaking. Part of the roof had been damaged by fallen branches. Suspicious, we examined the garage. Sure enough, the ceiling was once more leaking.

Now the garage represents a good half of our Service area. I strengthened the area in my office above the garage and began to attract the correct workmen. As I've discussed, in order for Fortunate Blessings to flourish, every single area of the house must be harmonious, especially Number Six. So it wasn't too surprising when David discovered a mistake had been made with his taxes. The Tax Department was demanding an amount which was clearly incorrect, but straightening things out was becoming a knotty problem.

Then one morning I met a wonderful man who was looking at the driveway next door. He'd been hired by my neighbor to put in a new driveway. He was straightforward. I liked him and his son who worked as his partner. Yes, they could fix the problems with the garage and put in a brick driveway. The price was reasonable. Then suddenly the ceiling of my office began to leak.

The leak was going all the way down to the basement and into the garage roof. David and I were desolate. There was no way around it. We called the roofers.

The moment the roof was repaired things began to move. Joe and Tony repaired the stone terrace and the garage roof. Better yet, the insurance from the ice storm paid for a large part of the damage. The men finished the brick driveway and David appeared home one night with the gift of a pair of stone lions. Tony and Joe built stone pillars for them, one either side of the driveway, an area which had always felt unprotected as the energy from the street came straight up the hill and into the driveway. We'd been talking about a pair of guardians ever since we'd moved in but we'd always chosen other priorities. Now our stone lions, Feng and Shui, were guarding the driveway. It felt completely different. A month later David received a call from the tax department. There had been a reassessment, nothing was owed at the present time. ❧

Chapter Twenty Nine

The Case of Pinocchio

As usual I knew nothing about my client, but this time the family wasn't even home. A cleaning lady let me in.

The basement of the townhouse had been converted into a children's playroom. There was a piano, baskets of stuffed toys, a train set and a television. Then something struck me as significant.

Hanging near the TV set was a toy Pinocchio, the wooden boy made by the toy maker Gepetto because he and his wife wanted a little boy. Pinocchio's nose, remember, has super-ordinary powers. Whenever he tells a lie the nose grows longer. The Pinocchio hanging from the ceiling of my client's basement had a VERY long nose. I detected blocks in Fortunate Blessings and stress in the Health areas.

When the family returned I said, "There is a situation to do with a person or people who should be of service. This could be a business associate or a family member. There has been deception and this is affecting both money flow and health."

It turned out my client's business partner had lied to him and double crossed him. This had created financial difficulties and a great deal of stress. I suggested Pinocchio be given away. Shortly afterwards my client went into a new line of work and prosperity once more began to flow.

Once again, Feng Shui had revealed a hidden problem with a remarkably direct and literal outer manifestation. ❧

Chapter Thirty

Nurturing the Creative Child: The Case of The Hangman's Noose

*T*he first tip that something was off-balance was seemingly as innocent as spring; a plant hanger attached to a side fence on the driveway of my client's property. But something about it disturbed me. I
squatted down and inspected the grass beneath. Sure enough there was
something white partially hidden by a bush. I reached in and brought
out a soggy wax drinking cup, the sort you buy at a fast food stand. This
particular one featured a picture of children on the side. They appeared
to be shouting to each other. While it was obvious the cup was intended to represent happy children at play, the expression on the face of one
of them was more a cry for help than a happy call. I looked at the picture for about a minute. Then I glanced up at the plant hanger. Why
wasn't there a pot or a plant in the holder? It was, after all, summer, and
the flowerbeds were well kept, filled with petunias and geraniums.

The planter was in the area of Number Seven, Childhood; the child
we have each been, any children in the family and the creativity within
each of us, the happy, playful, creative child.

The more I looked at that plant hanger the more it took on the form
of a hangman's gallows. Together with the screaming child on the cup
who was intended to be playing with its peers happily, I was immediately suspicious. The child had been damaged in some way.

When I explored the house I discovered inside a clothes closet, a
doorway which had been permanently closed, ostensibly to make more
room for shelving. In the bedroom was a whole wall of childhood
memorabilia, more than I usually find in my clients' houses. Baskets of
cute stuffed toys filled several corners, yet I didn't pick up the energy of
any actual children. It was as though the child had wistfully tried to create what it had been deprived of; the stuffed animals and the collection
of china dolls carried the energy of the past. The placement of a picture

of autumn leaves, one of a house in winter and a collection of butterflies, carefully pinned to a board and displayed in a glass case were my final clues. There was every evidence that a child had been abused. I was reluctant to open what Feng Shui suggested was an old pain.

I gave a very careful reading and was distressed when my client burst into tears. "That's exactly right," she sobbed. "I was an abused child. First my father, then my stepfather. I don't want to discuss it. I've been in therapy for years."

Now Feng Shui, as I've mentioned, is not therapy. There is no need to drag out every distressing detail of the past with my clients. While frequently, as part of the Feng Shui process, a client will discover the ideal counselor or therapist, the art of Feng Shui is primarily about unblocking energy through work with the physical environment. Having established that the reading was accurate we went on to unblock energy.

My client called six weeks later to tell me that she'd had all sorts of dreams about childhood, disturbing nightmares, actually. "They've stopped," she said. "I had my first happy dream last night and I've enrolled in art classes. I always wanted to paint."

This was a big step for her. At our initial appointment I'd asked, "What do you do for fun?"

"I can't think of anything," she replied. "Maybe eat ice cream."

For the first time in years she was beginning to play, to create. I was almost as excited as she was.

Inevitably Number Seven and Number Three go hand in hand; Childhood and Family. ❦

Chapter Thirty One

The Case of The Two Children

*B*eneath the New Mexican sun, Gabriela's pink adobe house looked like something from a travel poster; turquoise shutters, red geraniums in the window boxes. The first thing that caught my attention was a painting in the hallway.

A large green horse filled the center. To the right, its rider, a knight in armor, faced a shadowy man who occupied the entire left side of the painting.

The knight appeared small and delicate compared to the faceless man, and though the face was protected by a steel visor, I was sure it was a woman.

Its placement in the Tai Chi of the house was significant. In a corner of the basement which represented Fortunate Blessings was one of those rattan chairs you hang from the ceiling. In it sprawled a Hallowe'en skeleton.

A grinning jack o' lantern swung from the ceiling beside a pile of suitcases in the area of Relationship.

In the area of Life Journey I pushed aside boxes of office equipment to enter a small room. I groped for the light switch but the bulb had burned out. The room felt very cold.

It was a relief to return to the bright rooms upstairs. The kitchen, in the area of The Child and Creativity, was orderly and immaculate, but the placement of the stove indicated a blockage relating to childhood and the ability to have fun.

There were small clues throughout the house that indicated constrictions with health and family, but it was in the office upstairs that I discovered my main clue.

The painting of children at play appeared, at first glance, innocent enough. A boy and a girl in party clothes played tag. But their expressions were the giveaway.

Only the little boy was having fun as he yanked the hem of her frilly dress. She looked frightened. Carefully I pieced together my clues.

When we sat down for the reading, I said, "Gabriela, some aspect of the feminine, the yin, has been suppressed to protect itself from a very strong yang influence. Let's take a look at the painting in your hall."

Together we stood in front of the green horse and knight facing the big man. "To cope with overpowering yang, yin has disguised herself as yang and has dealt with the situation with great courage. But as long as the feminine is suppressed, the life journey will not allow full creativity and fun. This imbalance of yin and yang also causes difficulty with health and relationship. It's as though there is imbalance in every aspect of your life." I stopped and we returned to sit in the living room. Then Gabriela said, "When I was born my father wanted a boy. Whenever I behaved like a little girl he'd ignore me or make fun of me but when I did boy things he praised me. My mother was a clairvoyant who gave readings and he was always putting her down for what she did. Finally she had a nervous breakdown. He told me it was caused by her work. Later on, I began to notice I had my mother's gift of intuition but I was afraid of it, what if I had a nervous breakdown too? So I suppressed that whole side of me. To please my father I became an engineer and went into his firm.

"Later, I developed health problems and had a hysterectomy. You're right, I always feel unbalanced and I feel there's something missing from my life."

As Gabriela worked on her Recipe, she began to unblock the suppressed yin energy. She decided to take time out from her work as an engineer and explore her creativity, beginning with a vacation to one of the South Pacific islands renowned for its sensuality.

Gradually, as she cultivated her intuition, she felt more balanced. Slowly she began to use her creativity to explore ways to make her work more fun. ✿

Chapter Thirty Two

Feng Shui and Children: The Case of The Titanic

Children seem to have an intuitive understanding of the principles of Feng Shui. Let's think back for a moment. I'll bet, at some time during your childhood you had a secret hideaway. Was it in the middle of the backyard, out there in the open where everyone could see you? I'll bet it wasn't. Chances are it was concealed under a table with a blanket spread over it, or up in a tree, or in a tucked away corner. You probably chose your own "belly of the dragon" site. I know I did; my tree house, my dungeon, each of my cubby houses was concealed where I could view someone approaching.

Children love color and their rooms are usually a rainbow hue of perfectly balanced elements.

But as we grow up and are influenced by the expectations of others there is often a subtle change.

Gloria was at school when I arrived at her house. Her mother told me I had her daughter's permission to look at her room. It was a sunny, appealing room, with lots of cuddly stuffed animals and whimsical watercolors on the walls. But the moment I saw the big poster for the film, *Titanic,* I knew Gloria was having difficulty at school. It was a combination of energy patterns; the poster fit together with energy blocks in the Relationship areas of both property and house and, because of three doorways in her room, one a patio door to the garden that might allow intruders to enter, the reading suggested the little girl was unable to get a thorough rest at night.

Her mother confirmed the findings.

"It's true. Ever since we moved here she's had trouble sleeping. She also has nightmares. And she's having a hard time making friends at school. She starts out fine, has a friend over to play, it goes on for a while, then the friend drops her."

125

Gloria agreed to get rid of the *Titanic* poster. Her mother curtained the patio doors and helped her daughter place the stuffed animals to "guard" at night. A month later I called to see how she was getting on.

"She's sleeping through the night," her mother told me. "And surprise, surprise, the kid at school who's been making my daughter's life miserable won't be coming back next term. Her family is moving. And Gloria's been invited to a sleep over this weekend."

Jason, the young son of another client also had trouble sleeping. Jason's parents' separation had been a difficult one, with much hostility. One Sunday night Jason returned from his father's house in tears. His father had yelled and yelled at him about something minor.

Jason began to have trouble getting to sleep and would often wake up two or three times a night. His mother called me.

"My brother said Feng Shui might help. I'm ready to do anything to help Jason."

I explained that I wouldn't be able to fly out to the west coast for a month or two, but maybe I could help by telephone. Suddenly I had an image of something opposite Jason's bed.

"Could there be something violent facing Jason when he's asleep," I asked. By now I'd simply accepted the "hunches" that occurred more and more frequently.

"I'll go and look," his mother told me. When she returned she said, "He keeps his little Pokémon characters on the bureau."

"What are Pokémon characters?"

"They're like cute little warriors."

Aha!

"Could you discuss this with Jason and see if he would be willing to relocate them?"

"I'll try."

When I next talked to her a few days later she said, "He doesn't want to move them. He says the leader can be good or bad."

I let it ride. In Feng Shui cures, if they're to be successful, they can never be imposed by someone else, they have to come from within. Another week went by before I heard from Jason's mother again.

"Jason didn't sleep well last night. He says he wants to move the Pokémons now."

When I next talked to the family, Jason's sleep patterns had returned to normal. ❧

Chapter Thirty Three

Experience: The Case of
The Dusty Piano

*E*xperience is frequently referred to in Feng Shui as Knowledge. Knowledge is the result of Experience. Experience, learning from mistakes, trusting our intuition, gives us the opportunity to apply insight and gain wisdom.

Most of us carry old pain from the past but what each of us does with that pain varies enormously. Some of us close the door on the past, as I did until my heart attack at age thirty, and prefer to "get on with" the future. Some of us spend years in therapy trying to make sense of our experience and move beyond it. When we examine the past until we gain insight, release it and move forward, using our insights to help ourselves and others, our energy begins to flow harmoniously in each of the other areas of our lives.

Joseph's Number Eight area on each of the three floors of his house contained storage. In the basement it was a closet crammed almost to the ceiling with "stuff." On the main floor a small study was equally congested — boxes of books, old prints, photographs. Upstairs the same area was a child's bedroom. Clearly the child had grown up and moved out some time ago leaving the usual bric-a-brac of adolescence — posters, a stereo, unplugged phone, a goose neck lamp and piles of old magazines. After a detailed examination of the house it was clear that the clogged areas were preventing Joseph's creativity from full expression.

In the living room, a seven-foot Steinway piano faced the wall in the area corresponding to Number Seven. When I ran my finger gently along the lid it left a mark in the dust. Blocked doorways and a sealed door to a patio off the kitchen indicated difficulty in relationships and, together with a list of smaller clues, the picture emerged clearly.

Joseph and his wife had separated some time ago. Their son had gone away to college and Joseph, an engineer with a passion for music and a talent for piano, hadn't opened the instrument in fourteen months.

As I've explained earlier, the order in which Feng Shui steps are approached is critical. An examination of Joseph's basement closet revealed the origin of the blocks. The boxes were filled with books on the Holocaust; photographs of Nazi atrocities, newspaper clippings about concentration camp survivors.

"My parents were Auschwitz survivors," Joseph told me after the assessment. "When I was growing up the house was full of things like photos of death camp skeletons. We had a whole cupboard of photos of atrocities. All my grandparents had died in the camps. My father had to watch his wife and baby daughter dragged away from him on a railway platform. He never saw them again.

"I hated the atmosphere in the house. It was dark and gloomy and nobody ever had any fun. But at the same time it was part of me. I grew up feeling guilty for being a survivor and having it so good. I wanted to be a pianist but my parents wanted their son to be the usual doctor, dentist or lawyer. We compromised on engineer.

"But no matter what I do it's like I'm always carrying this nasty dark part of me everywhere I go."

Joseph agreed to follow the steps in the recipe I drew up precisely but it wasn't easy. It took him a year to clear out the closet, study and his son's room. And he had disturbing nightmares and feelings of depression. Fortunately, he decided to also go for counseling. At the end of a year we spoke.

"I feel lighter, like all these dark things happened in my past and are over and I can get on with things now. The moment I turned the piano so I could see the doorway I could actually feel the shift in energy. I've started playing again and I'm excited about music again for the first time in ages." ✤

Chapter Thirty Four

Illumination: The Case of The Reverse Mirrors

This area of the Bagua is also referred to as Fame and Reputation. I prefer Illumination, because this is the end product of harmony between the other eight areas — we do what we love to do and find our "path." This creates a good relationship with ourselves, therefore with others, which in turn is the basis for loving family relationships and vigorous good health. The combination of these creates many fortunate blessings which contribute to a strong core. This allows us to contribute to those around us and accept service from others. The resultant creativity encourages us to explore ideas, to sift through our experience and apply insight; to learn and to share our insights via teaching. As a result of this process we are truly able to access our inner light, which in turn illuminates those around us. In return the universe honors us for our authentic selves. This is my interpretation of fame and reputation!

Clearly, when there is an energy constriction in Number One, Life Journey/Career, there will be corresponding blocks in Number Nine, Illumination. For example, if we are working in an area just to make money, but we're not passionate about our job, this will show in our life journey area. Correspondingly, Number Nine will contain a block.

Helen and Ted's house was beautiful, with a small pond by the front door, fed by a gentle waterfall. The direction of the flow was towards the front door feeding good energy into the house. Inside were healthy plants and lots of sunshine. The home was tastefully furnished with very little clutter.

At first glance it seemed the Chi was flowing extremely well. However, I continued my snoop and creep. The garden contained birdhouses and another fountain. I stood in the sun and relaxed to the gentle splashing of water. Then something about the fountain struck me. It was made from a large pot with small holes in the side, flowing into a dish below. It was the direction of the water that caught my attention. Two streams of water were flowing towards the house, two away from it.

I continued my examination of the garden and paused near the vegetable garden. Leaning against the fence was a long mirror. When I stood in front of it I could see my legs and body but no head.

Now a large mirror placed outside a house is the exception rather than the rule. Nor was it something that just happened to be there; this was an orderly house.

Both the mirror and the fountain were placed in the area of Illumination. The placement of well-tended bird feeders indicated to me that the people in the house were generating light within from doing things they loved to do. However, the flow of the fountain, half towards the house, half away from it, together with the mirror reflecting back towards the house indicated to me that there was an ambivalence about how much they choose to have their light go out into the world, attracting recognition.

As I completed my assessment I discovered a vital piece of the puzzle. The area of creativity contained two studios, his and hers. His contained energy that clearly aimed for recognition, while hers presented contradictions; the room was filled with beautiful fabrics — it was clear she was a designer, and a very good one. Yet one of her work areas was back to the door. And in the corner behind some storage was a door.

I opened it; inside was a small room piled high with so many objects it was difficult to enter. This gave me my final clue.

It was apparent that Ted loved what he did; designing and making fine jewelry. He was clear about wanting recognition, symbolized by the part of the fountain flowing outwards. The mirror had been placed in this area to activate recognition. However, instead of getting the light out into the world it was bounced back to the house along with Helen's part of the fountain!

When I described the pattern to them both they agreed.

"I'm just coming out of a period where I was very successful and had a lot of recognition," Helen told me. "I've been sort of hibernating for the past year, but I feel I need to move in another direction... I'm not sure what it is."

Both Helen and Ted wanted to increase the flow of money. In order to do this the mixed messages needed to be addressed and the creativity unblocked.

The results were astonishing. Six months later, not only were Ted's earnings way up, Helen had discovered a new career which nine months later brought her international recognition as well as money to do whatever she chose! 🐉🐉

Chapter Thirty Five

The Case of The Two Doors

*W*hen Leonie and Gerry invited me to Feng Shui their house I was surprised. Both talented healers, I more or less assumed they didn't need a reading. Well, maybe it was just curiosity.

They lived on a large piece of country property with orchards and healthy vegetable gardens.

As I walked beneath the budding fruit trees and along the carefully tended paths I relaxed a little, this wouldn't take long, their energies were great. Then I noticed that the ends of a barbed wire fence had been looped over the fence pole near the entrance. From that moment on I forgot about the birdsong and spring buds.

Nose to the ground, so to speak, I was on the trail. In the farthest corner of the property, in Relationship, half covered by long grass stood a piece of rusted farm equipment I couldn't identify. Inside, piled among old strips of metal was more barbed wire. The potting shed and pole barn were well tended. Yet behind the shed, in Family and Health was a pile of logs, the bottom one attached to a pair of hauling chains.

The house was bright, cheerful and well-tended.

Just inside the front door, in the Children's area was an oil painting of an ocean; big waves breaking over rocks. Fortunate Blessings was a pair of storage rooms; in the first, the doorway opened only halfway, blocked by the washing machine. In the second, the door was propped open by boxes of dog food; it was unable to close.

In Knowledge, half the garage was filled with an old mattress, a chair with its back to the door, and a pile of other cast off possessions. Illumination was plunk in the middle of the kitchen sink.

"Leonie and Gerry, the energy in your house is high and beautiful; you are generous and there is much love," I began. "However, there has been trauma with the mother and pain with the father; the period between age 10 and 15 has been especially difficult. The child has not been supported, this has created low self-esteem and confidence which makes it difficult to let the light go out into the world fully. It's as though the energy is saying, I'm not good enough. This is brought about by old difficulty from the past, childhood which has been locked away. It has created the ability to give, give, give, but not to be able to receive. This limits financial income and feelings of self worth."

"My mother gave me away when I was born," Leonie told me close to tears. "And when I was nine until I turned fifteen life was hell. You're right, I've never felt good enough and I have trouble asking for payment for my services. Sometimes I work three or four hours without being paid even my hourly rate."

"My father was, let's say, very strict," Gerald told me. "If I did what I wanted I knew I'd pay for it when I got home."

The next time I spoke to Leonie after many of the changes had been done, she told me, "I'm feeling different. Clearer and more sure of myself. And a health problem I've had for years has started to clear up. It's like I don't need it any more."

Chapter Thirty Six

The Case of The Burning House

Michael's apartment was about as minimalist as they come; one of those white on white high-rises with a breathtaking view of the city, and at night the lights would be spectacular.

My assessment didn't take long; there was so little there! However, it was apparent that while there was a lively ambition, the end product wasn't up to expectations. How did I reach this conclusion?

The entrance door was in the area of Career, which opened into a small foyer. The white walls held three black and white photographs; each of a lily. Now, while the Career area is the element of water, enhanced by the water of the glass and by the black and white (black represents water, white metal, which nurtures water), the shape of a lily is triangular. This corresponds with the fire element, the element of Illumination. The apartment was one big open room, with a sleeping/bathroom alcove. While the walls and furniture were white, the views featured by day, skyscrapers and a building with a pyramid-shaped top, rather like a rocket, indicated an abundance of fire and the possibility for recognition in a big way. By night, the sea of lights of the city also provided an abundance of fire.

There was one little glitch. Smack in the middle of the area of Illumination hung a large black and white photograph of a city on fire. Skyscrapers burned grotesquely while below an army of firefighters aimed their hoses without effect.

Now why would Michael sabotage the success he deserved? He had received some recognition for his black and white photographs, but not the recognition he wanted. His work was good, very, very good, yet something was holding him back.

The clues were right there in Relationship as well as Health and Family. Over the bed hung another photograph, a sunrise over a tropical island. But instead of the light radiating into the morning, it was completely blocked by a mass of clouds so dark it was almost black. In the kitchen, the placement of knives confirmed my suspicions. And there was one further clue.

The bathroom was in the area of Creativity. Along the wall hung three more photographs; the first was a waterfront with a gathering of people who appeared happy. The second was the same waterfront, but this time a man had climbed into the boat and was rowing away, the crowd waving. The third picture was a back view of a figure clad in black, taken from behind against snow covered mountains which dwarfed the figure completely.

"Michael, the energy patterns seem to indicate that your father left you and your mother when you were a child. This was somehow related to his pursuit of a dream, but left you feeling abandoned. You appear to be doing work you love, you're following your bliss, but this has created difficulty for you in relationship and, for you, recognition is something which although you want it, represents the destruction of family life and relationship."

It turned out Michael's father was a well-known writer who was always in search of a new place to live.

"He loved to move and the more famous he became the less we saw of him. He'd take off for months at a time, he said he had to move to write. I was known as the son of "X." All my friends respected me just because I was his son, but Dad was never there. All I wanted was to do the things my friends did, corny stuff like go to a ball game with their dads. Finally, he left us and remarried.

"When I became a photographer I started to understand my dad. When I'm printing I need hours to myself, not just in the darkroom but to just think. I married a woman and we had a daughter. Part of me wanted to spend time with them but part of me felt trapped, like I couldn't just take off anymore. She divorced me three years ago. I don't want a relationship right now but I feel my career's not moving the way it should."

The "cure" was straightforward. After a simple recipe to balance the energy in each area of his apartment, he completed the final step by replacing the burning city with a dramatic photograph of the pyramid topped Sears building in Chicago to bring in the fire element and allow him to get his light out into the world. Before the year was out,

Michael's work was displayed at New York's prestigious Whitney Museum. He hasn't looked back since. ✺

Chapter Thirty Seven

The Case of The Cat Litter Box

In the Service area of Ingrid's apartment was the staircase to the basement. At the foot of the stairs hung a large dartboard bristling with darts. I was not surprised to find the cat litter box in the area of Illumination!

When we sat down I said, "Ingrid, you're not getting as much help from the people you work with as you need, in fact it's possible that somebody is bad talking you."

As it turned out, Ingrid was a nurse at a busy city hospital.

"I love my patients, but my supervisor's making my life miserable. I've tried getting along with her but she really seems to have it in for me. I'm thinking of looking for another job."

I suggested she relocate the cat litter. That wasn't so easy.

"Molesworth would hate that," Ingrid told me, stroking the enormous black cat on her lap. He looked at me with brilliant green eyes. Finally, she decided to move the litter pan one inch a day. She replaced the dartboard with a picture of harp-playing angels. That was easy and so were some of the other changes that included removing a knife block from the kitchen counter and turning her desk to face the door. As the weeks passed. Molesworth's litter inched down the hall and into the utility room. Ingrid called me, delighted.

"The most amazing thing has happened! My supervisor's pregnant and she's quitting — and she's not coming back. The new supervisor's a woman I really like. I'm so happy, I can't tell you...!"

Chapter Thirty Eight

Adventures With Real Estate:
The Case of The Burial Pit

*D*avid and I were considering putting our Montreal house on the market. I figured our best bet was to find a realtor familiar with the principles of Feng Shui. Now at this point, the words Feng Shui in Montreal were as meaningful as "Ugga Wugga." My friends, on learning that I was no longer a childbirth educator, nor a writer, were less than enthusiastic about my new career. They figured I'd lost it, joined the New Age. While one or two were curious, others pointedly refrained from asking me what I was doing. I think it embarrassed them. Energy was something you expended at the gym, not something you measured by creeping around strangers' houses.

Several considered it enormously amusing and lost no chance to tease me. So I became a closet Feng Shui practitioner, known only by a sort of underground client to client. Nor were my clients initially enthusiastic. Several times during an initial phone contact they'd say things like, "I don't really believe in Feng Shui, but my friend told me I should try it. I guess it can't do any harm."

While I wracked my brains for an appropriate realtor I recalled an open house I'd attended a year or so previously. It was a fine old Victorian stone house with a coach house. I am addicted to coach houses and can identify every single one in Montreal. When I asked the realtor, a Chinese woman, if I could see inside the coach house she told me bluntly, "No. I'm showing the house right now and I don't think the owner would want me to give you the key."

I found her bluntness refreshing. We chatted for a few moments and she told me her background was in architecture. Now, looking for an appropriate realtor, I remembered her. I decided she seemed like the right agent for my house, although I hadn't seen her name on any of the properties for sale in my immediate area. She was bright, she was direct, and she probably knew about Feng Shui, I reasoned. After all, she was Chinese.

Patricia Chang and I sat in my living room, Colonel Olney's original room with it's view of the city stretching down to the river. It's one of my favorite rooms. In the bay window we installed a window seat flanked by floor-to-ceiling bookshelves. The furniture's an eclectic mix of comfortable chintz slip-covered sofas, a deep red velvet wing back chair, a pair of red, yellow and blue oriental print chairs and a pair of sky blue over-stuffed chaises longues. An antique tea trolley, some big paintings and lots of books create a room you just relax into, ideal for parties, one of those rooms that "feels" right.

Patricia was taking it all in, but remained inscrutable. She was impeccably groomed and wore a pink suit. Her delicate shoes made my own size nines feel big and clumpy; I have an extra bone on the back of my right foot, called a calcaneal spur, and the only shoes I'm comfortable in are things like Birkenstocks, soft canvas boots, and high-top running shoes. One of David's small regrets is I can't wear the elegant Italian leather shoes he's fond of.

"I like your house," she finally pronounced. "It has good flow for entertaining."

I asked her about Feng Shui.

"I've heard about it, but I really don't know much. I was born and raised in Boston. My parents are Chinese but they don't believe in Feng Shui. They think it's a bunch of old superstition."

Patricia may not have known much about it but she was curious. I liked her and decided she was the person I'd been looking for.

"Whether or not you decide to have me sell your house, I'd like you to come and look at my place," she said abruptly. I liked the way her eyes sparkled. She seemed completely present and focused. We agreed on a time the following week.

Patricia owned a unit in the Habitat complex designed for Expo '67 by architect Moishe Safdie. It's always reminded me of an urban pueblo, in fact if you compare photographs of the Taos Pueblo with Habitat you'll see a lot in common; they both straggle freely like a child's castle of blocks, a series of interlocking walkways, views and exciting angles. Of course, the Taos pueblo is built from mud-and-straw adobe blocks while Habitat is made of pre-cast concrete. Both structures, however, share an exciting relationship with space. Just moments from downtown Montreal, Habitat sits between two bodies of water with glorious views of the city skyline. It's nestled in a greenbelt with large fountains correctly located in the Number One, Life Journey area in front of the complex. Naturally it attracts people with interesting and creative careers.

When I had finished my snoop and creep of Patricia's unit we sat down and I gave her my assessment, as usual asking her to comment. She seemed surprised at its accurate description of her life. We went through the recipe, even including a few changes for her storage locker.

Several times in the next month, she called to discuss details.

As she began to notice changes in her life she asked me to take a look at one of her listings, the most hopeless in her opinion, as it had been on the market for two years. The owner had moved out and was living in New York.

Doing Feng Shui on an empty house is interesting; you have a chance to assess the property and house as it affects rather than the interaction of how it both affects and reflects the people who live there. Naturally I knew nothing of the owner.

The location was attractive; a quiet cul de sac on the side of Montreal's Mount Royal, an easy walk downtown, with good city views. The rooms were bright and spacious. However, there was a curious scooped out area of the lawn. The vibration reflected Relationships; it was almost like an ancient burial pit. Curious.

The area of Number Four, Fortunate Blessings, contained a steep stone staircase through a patch of woodland down to the property line. It didn't seem to have a purpose as the area below was overgrown. Moreover, the stairs were in bad repair; some of the stones were broken, and either side of the staircase lay stones which had once formed a low retaining wall, terracing the slope.

The kitchen, located in Number Six, service, contained an oddly shaped counter with a pointed edge that formed an arrow as you entered. The energies raced through from the front door down a hallway and out a window, leaving no time to collect and center in Number Five. Sharp stones in the area beyond the "burial pit" completed my suspicions.

"There has been pain in relationship," I told Pat. "It's almost as though something has died and the fortunate blessings have crumbled. People who should have been helpful have presented problems and the energy has simply left the house."

In her direct way, Pat informed me that yes, there had been a tragedy and a death on the property and the owner had decided to leave.

After I made my recommendations, she phoned the owner, asking permission to make the changes. She agreed. While normally I do not participate in changes as this is the creation and process of the owner, I made an exception in this case. Pat wanted to have an open house very soon before the weather turned, Montreal-like, icy. Already the first leaves were falling, collecting in forlorn piles near the front door. I offered to help position the fallen stones by the back staircase.

Within the week, the "burial pit" which, it turned out, had once contained a swimming pool when the owner bought the house, was filled in and re-sodded. The stone steps were repaired and the area cleaned out and terraced. Sharp objects were removed and the kitchen softened by the placement of plants. The rapid ebb of energy in the hallway we corrected by placing a vase of silk poppies in an alcove, together with an oriental rug on the dark wooden floor.

Immediately the energy felt better.

The house sold in record time.

From then on, Patricia asked me do an assessment for each of her listings. Rarely did I meet the owners, but Pat began to tell me how, as they made the changes, their lives began to improve.

At the same time she was noticing improvements in her own life.

And I was having fun. Suddenly, I'd found a person who believed in what I was doing and who had a dry and delightful sense of humor. We laughed a lot.

I appreciated her frankness and honesty. Once, after a day when I'd looked at three properties with her, I told her I didn't think I could do the final property justice. She picked up her car phone and dialed the owner. "We can't make it today, sorry. The Feng Shui expert's tired!"

When Pat discovers something she shares it with her many friends. Within a month my phone was ringing constantly with her referrals. Concerned about the well-being of each member of her family, we'd confer on ways to help each one. We had many delightful conversations.

I left for the winter, but Pat and I kept in touch. Her listings were increasing and she was selling houses one after another, reaching the goals she had written down at our initial meeting.

Code Purple

For the first year of my practice I assumed that my ability to "diagnose" my clients' energy patterns was simply the gift of a competent detective. After all, since I was seven years old I'd been honing my skills of observation, starting with Kim's Game.

A Feng Shui practitioner is a master of the intuitive. Application of the principles, in my opinion, comprises about 40 percent of the skills. The rest is intuition, the ability to compute a multitude of impressions simultaneously. And each practitioner works differently. Naturally, the most important thing is that you are able to help your client improve her or his life.

Sometimes a client would ask if I were psychic.

"No," I'd reply, "I'm just a good detective."

For some reason I didn't want to be considered psychic. After all, my background in physiotherapy was scientific, and though I'd journeyed deeply into the New Age world in my quest for a healing, I was wary of people who claimed to have supernatural powers. Although I had met genuine healers and psychics like my friend Marie-France, I didn't want to be one. Then along came an experience to challenge that.

My telephone rang one morning. It was a woman in Virginia.

"Could you possibly fly down here and look at my house?"

"I'm sorry, I can't get away for at least a month."

When I suggested she find a practitioner in her own area she sounded disappointed.

Suddenly I heard myself say, "The problem is in the basement. There's something sharp in the left corner of the basement that represents difficulty with the parents at the age of four. Our parents are our earliest support people. When we fail to get support it weakens our energies. This undermines our ability to do what we love and believe that we can earn a living from it. This has produced confusion. In order for recognition of the authentic self, it would be advisable to throw out the sharp object in the basement."

There was silence at the other end. What on earth had I been ranting on about? "Are you there?" I asked, embarrassed.

"Yes. I'm on my portable phone and I'm just walking down the stairs into the basement. Oh my God, there's a big broken mirror here. It's exactly where you said it was."

I heard myself say, "Could you stand in front of it and tell me what part of your body you see?"

"I can just see my legs from the knees down."

"Can you move forward without a head?"

"No."

"The placement of the mirror would indicate that the child has been helpless to move forward. I'd suggest you get rid of the mirror, it's partly broken in the bottom right corner, isn't it?"

"Yes. The bottom right corner's broken off."

"And if you send me photos of each room perhaps we can make some other changes."

When I put down the phone I sat very still for a long time. What was going on? How could I possibly have known about the mirror? Was Marie-France correct and I actually had some paranormal ability? If so, I didn't want it. It was one thing to be a good detective, I was proud of that gift; it was acceptable. But now I felt like a witch! I resolved never to let my clients know about this ability.

Then one Sunday Pat Chang called me in the southwest from Montreal.

"Hi, I'm at a property on Cote St. Antoine Road. The house has been on the market a long time. They had one offer but it fell through. I wanted to run a few things by you and see if you could make some suggestions."

"Sure. Can you walk me through."

She began to describe the house on her cell phone, moving from room to room. Suddenly, without thinking about it I heard myself say, "The problem is in the basement. If you go down there you'll find something that's turning things sour."

A few moments later she confirmed this. "Yes, there are bottles of vinegar down here. I'll tell the owner to move them. Anything else?"

"Yes. In the back left of the house there's something sharp... inside, not out."

"I'm on my way. No, there's nothing sharp here. It's a sun room off the kitchen. It's a nice room, lots of plants and sun."

I was insistent.

"There's something sharp. Keep looking."

Then I heard her sort of gasp. "You're right. There's a painting on the wall of a couple of green apples with a knife beside them."

"Get rid of them."

"Where?"

"In a closet." I named the area of the house.

"Anything else?"

"Yes." There was no hesitation. "Outside in the far left there's something blocked."

"Oh, that's the garage. I'll take a look." A few minutes later I heard her laugh. "It's full of stuff, OK, I know, get them to clear it out, right?"

"Right."

The house, one plagued by the location problem of a gas station next door, sold shortly after for an excellent price. Patricia told me that some business difficulties the owner had been wrestling with had been solved. Hmmm.

From this point on she'd simply call me and give me the address. Right away I could sense where the difficulty was. But how did I know? I've never considered myself psychic, Marie-France's predictions in Taos notwithstanding. Other people dreamed visionary dreams, whizzed through the night in their astral bodies. Not I. So how was I to explain my ability to sense the energies of houses I hadn't seen?

I chose not to explain it. Even though I was aware that my gift for helping women in childbirth was a blend of intuition and scientific skills, my rational, scientific training as a physiotherapist protested at this new turn of events.

I knew I couldn't ignore it. One afternoon I was speaking to Merlinda, a client who had worked with Feng Shui in her office. She'd noticed improvements in many areas but "I'm still having trouble with my mother. We're still arguing."

I heard myself say, "There's something sharp out on your roof. Open your window and have a look."

"Hang on. I'm opening the window and climbing out." I heard her giggle.

"You're right. There are a bunch of nails out here."

After that she and her mother improved their relationship considerably. I could picture friends' faces if they knew that not only was I a Feng Shui practitioner but was now giving "readings" on the phone! So I told nobody. Only Patricia suspected. From this time on, whenever I "knew," we jokingly referred to it as "Code Purple."

Code Purple turned out to expand the scope of my practice. Up until then I had confined my consultations to on location. Then a woman called from Chicago and asked if I could do her apartment. Rather than fly to Chicago, I suggested she send me a floor plan and photographs.

As I talked to her I could sense in which area of her life the difficulties lay. This was confirmed by the photographs.

She agreed, and proceeded to make changes. On completion she called, delighted.

"My whole life has changed. I feel much clearer and in control. And my work is going so much better. I seem to be attracting all sorts of Helpful People."

The more I've thought about Code Purple, the more I'm inclined to believe that as we work with energy we develop the ability to gain information energetically. Because our universe is holographic, the house in one city generates an energy pattern which can be sensed from anywhere in the world. Perhaps it's a little like the unseen waves of telecommunications. Certainly it's a whole lot more comfortable than air travel!

Chapter Thirty Nine

Feng Shui at McGill University: The Case of The Clocks

By this time Pat and I were working together constantly and she was becoming increasingly interested in the potential of Feng Shui, telling every single person about it and how it was changing her life. She had paid off a large debt, her listings were selling, but the most important change was the way she felt. She began to write her book, *Humor and Hope for Humanity*.

Pat's enthusiasm is contagious. Suddenly people were talking about Feng Shui all over Montreal.

I was contacted by Juliette Patterson and Erica Goldstein, graduates of the McGill University School of Architecture. Would I be able to give a public lecture and a workshop for architects?

This was exciting. The opportunity to link Feng Shui where I believe it belongs, with architecture and design, was, I felt a step in the right direction. Feng Shui is at its most basic, an extremely practical building code.

The opportunity to reach architects as well as spread the word publicly was an attractive one. Of course, it was Pat who had given Juliette and Erica my name. That summer Pat and I looked at house after house together. She worked with the owners to make the changes, often calling me to ask things like, "Where do we get a hanging plant long enough to cover the corner of a house?" or "I can't find a rainbow windsock for my parents backyard so I hung one of my scarves out there and my mother's worried the neighbors will think they're weird!"

We continued to laugh a lot. And the houses kept on selling.

I prowled the city taking photos of buildings for my slide presentation in September. The organizers were nervous about not having a full house. I was sure it would have the right number of people. After all, Feng Shui is about bringing in Many Fortunate Blessings. How could I doubt it?

The morning of the public lecture, a local radio station called for an interview on a program called "Daybreak." The host, Dave Bronstetter, at the end of our interview, asked, "When you recommend changes, can companies see this in their bottom line?"

I assured him they could and did.

"What's your response when people just say it's bunk?"

"I think it's good to be cynical. You don't have to believe in it to get results, you just have to make the changes."

The afternoon of the lecture which we'd titled "The Validity of Feng Shui in Architectural Practice," I was nervous. After all, I hadn't been on the lecture circuit in a big way since prior to my heart attack. The last lecture I'd given, apart from book tours for the novels, had been on parents' rights in childbirth and the birthing room concept. Those days seemed a hundred years away. What if I'd lost my edge? As I arranged and rearranged my slides I realized I'd become shy. Apart from my Feng Shui consultations I live a very private life with David, our menagerie and a handful of close friends. Suddenly I was terrified.

As part of my preparation for the lecture I had prowled the McGill campus, photographing familiar buildings, but though I've taught obstetrics to second and third year students in the School of Physical and Occupational therapy for twenty years, I began to look at the familiar buildings through new eyes.

Grand gates mark the entrance of the McGill campus from elegant Sherbrooke Street. As I examined the two pillars either side I had a revelation; the clocks in each pillar had stopped. When I mentioned this to David he replied, "Oh yes, I don't think they were working even when I went to school there."

Those clocks mark the Number One area of the university; its Life Journey. At the turn of the century, McGill was world-famous, particularly for Medicine and Law. The last twenty years however have seen a gradual decline in funding. Facilities have struggled to stay alive, budgets have been slashed. Moreover, when I examined the campus I found windows and doors overgrown with ivy, another sure sign that the Chi was down on its luck.

The School of Architecture is a handsome old stone building with fine proportions and a pair of stone lions guarding the front steps. However, the day of the lecture I was dismayed to discover the steps boarded over for repairs, and a sign rerouting us to a side entrance.

Not good Chi. But David Covo, Dean of the school rose superbly to the occasion. A believer in Feng Shui, he had enthusiastically supported the event at every phase, arriving the night before as we set up the room for the workshop, moving furniture, positioning screens and big plants. He'd even had the windows cleaned until they sparkled. He promised the front door would be available. And it was. A friend of Patricia Chang's who owned the wonderful garden store, Chameleon Vert, had donated large flowering red plants to bring good Chi to the platform.

The lecture was at six. At 5:15 pm people started arriving, hordes of them. They just kept coming and coming until there wasn't a seat left in the auditorium. Some sat on the steps high up. Others crowded around the doors. There was no admission fee. As a result there was a complete cross-section of people, old people, students and everyone in between. My stomach turned queasy for a moment and I headed for the bath-room, notes in hand.

When I returned. David Covo introduced me. The audience was very quiet. Among the hundreds of faces looking down at me from the steeply pitched auditorium were the encouraging ones of friends, clients and, of course, David. Marie-France and her friend Paul were smiling at me. My friend Elaine Wasserman had before the lecture said, "Just look at me. I'll smile back and you'll be fine."

And I was. I relaxed. The words came through with clarity. "How many of you built a cubby house when you were a child?" I began. Nearly every hand in the auditorium went up. "How many built a tree-house? A cubby under a table or in a dark and secret place?" Another show of hands.

"How many of you built one in the middle of the backyard?" Not a hand. "You were demonstrating the universal principles of Feng Shui, the ancient Chinese Art of Placement," I told them. "The instinctive urge to position our dwellings in a safe place where we can see anyone approaching. The original Feng Shui practitioners, the Taoist monks, referred to this siting as the "belly of the dragon."

The slides flashed on the screen; Hong Kong with the harbor in front in the area of Water/Life Journey; Montreal, the river in front, Mount Royal behind; the Aboriginal cave of Arnhem Land in Northern Australia with its commanding view of the flood plane below; a man reading a newspaper in a café. Though he's the only person there he's positioned himself in a corner, back to the wall with a view of the entire room. The audience was very quiet. I could tell they were enjoying the show. So was I. We went through slides of houses and buildings around the world, then explored the various schools of Feng Shui and the underlying principles of Chi flow, balance of elements and yin and yang. Then I outlined "cases" and finished with nine pointers we can all use in our houses to balance and move the Chi. I had saved my slides of the McGill Gates until the end.

"The placement of the stopped clocks would indicate a slowing of the life force and career."

A murmur of agreement ran through the crowd. The evening concluded with a panel of architects with various experiences and knowledge of Feng Shui, a philosophical discussion which generated all sorts of stimulating questions from the audience.

Sixty three design professionals attended the workshop the next day. The Chi was high and we had a wonderful time.

Then the exciting changes began to happen. It seemed everyone was talking about Feng Shui. Radio and TV producers began to phone. But the change which gave me most pleasure occurred a month later. My husband David's book of short stories, *Relative Exposures,* co-authored with Torben Schioler, launched at a local bookstore on an evening in October. Paragraph is directly opposite McGill University and as I parked my car I looked up and witnessed a small miracle. The clocks. Each of them was keeping time! ෴

Chapter Forty

More Small Miracles

*A*lmost every day a client calls to tell me about the changes in his or her life which follow the completion of the changes. Yesterday Gillian called.

"I don't know if this always happens but I've been sleeping more soundly than I can remember, since I started the recipe. And I've been having so many dreams. A friend gave me a dictionary of dreams and I looked up all the symbols I've remembered from the dreams. Every one of them is a good omen. I feel completely wonderful. Each time I begin a change in the recipe you gave me I think about it and it seems so obvious. The most difficult thing is to do the changes in order and not go too fast. I'm almost sorry I'm just about finished."

Birgitte called to say, "Since you neutralized the Hartmann Lines I notice a huge difference. My two sons used to come into the house and they'd always argue right there in the living room where the line was. And I had this tense feeling in my stomach whenever I came into the house from the garage where the line was. That's gone. Right after you left, the boys came home and they helped me unload the groceries from the car. I asked them, 'Do you notice any difference in here' and they said, 'it feels sort of calm.'"

Phil called, "You know you said the garbage chute outside my apartment was draining my career. Well, I made the change and I want to tell you, a magazine called and they're doing a feature on me!"

A few weeks ago I was invited to Feng Shui a small pastry shop. Revenue was so bad they were considering bankruptcy. After the assessment they were eager to complete the changes. Today I learned about their first wonderful "out of the blue." The owner and his wife had attended a relative's christening party at a major hotel chain. He'd taken some trays of his own pastries and a cake. It was a wonderful party and afterwards the management approached him and asked, "Where did you get those pastries?"

"I made them."

"We might be interested in having you supply us."

Feng Shui works from the roots up. As you remove old blockages you create harmony. From harmony come the Fortunate Blessings including the money to do as you choose. Money doesn't usually just fall from the sky, or does it?

Recently one of my clients invited me in for a tune-up. It was a year since our initial consultation.

"It took a long time to clear out all the old blockages," she told me. "It wasn't easy. It seemed to take forever before I could get to some of the parts associated with childhood and my family. But the moment I did the most incredible thing happened. I've waited until you were here to tell you this because you have to see it to believe it. Let's go out in the garden."

I followed her into the sunshine. She had a beautiful backyard filled with spring blossoms. A big yellow butterfly hovered nearby. She stopped in front of a trellis and reached into a small pot for a folded piece of paper.

"Right after I did that last change in my Childhood area, I drove home one afternoon and there was a piece of paper on my lawn," she said mysteriously as she unfolded the paper and handed it to me.

In the top left corner in big print was the word "free." In big letters below it said "$10,000."

I didn't have my glasses and couldn't read the small print, but it looked like one of those special offer circulars.

As I read, my client blurted, "Two days later my aunt phoned to say she was giving me $10,000!"

Perhaps the most poignant of Feng Shui miracles was Abigail. A woman in her forties, her relationship with her mother had been difficult, as long as she could remember. Following her recipe of changes brought up many painful memories. At first nothing much in her life appeared to change. I didn't hear from her for several months. Then one evening she called. "I can't believe this. Remember how I told you my mother and I were getting on a bit better. Well, I went home for a visit and it's the first really nice time I can remember having with her." She paused. Then, in a shaky voice she blurted, "My mother told me she loves me. It's the first time in my life. And remember I told you she always used to say giving money to me was like throwing it into a hole in the ground? Well, she's offered me money to help me start my business." 🐾

Chapter Forty One

Principles Not Rules: The Case of The Star-Shaped Mirror

*I*t's not unusual for my clients, many of whom have picked up bits and pieces of Feng Shui here and there, to say things like, "A friend told me I should leave the front door light on 24-hours a day," or "Someone told me I shouldn't have a mirror here," or "My partner and I have just split. A friend called to tell me it was because of the position of the bed."

While Feng Shui does operate on a basis of logical principles, these are just that, principles, not rules. This was brought home to me recently in a wonderful gift of clarity. I had been called into the home of a lovely woman who, as she put it, had had, "nothing but trouble since I moved in here."

She'd looked forward to the move to a new neighborhood and had the house built according to her design.

"I'm wondering if it's haunted," she told me on the phone. "A friend told me the energy on the land is bad. Maybe I should move. I want you tell me if it's better to move out?" I said that I never tell people to move. That's not my role.

Frequently clients have me look at land or houses or office space they're thinking of buying. This is quite different. They have options.

One hot Sunday morning I looked at several different properties with a young couple searching for their first house. The first one we drove up to had a combination of several design difficulties which would involve considerable correction. I told them so. We looked at another five or six places but there was always one reason or another to be wary. The final house, though, was perfect. In the same way, I often work with families choosing pieces of land, or architects siting houses. We want to go for the very best possible in these situations. But when someone has already invested a large amount of money and effort in building her dream home, I believe in doing everything possible to heal the house.

However, when I arrived at the home of the woman who'd asked me if she should move, my heart sank. The poor woman could scarcely walk. "I had a back problem when I came here," she told me as we introduced ourselves and I met her three charming little dogs and two cats, "but it's been getting worse and worse since I've been here. Nothing's gone right. I've had problems with the contractor and money problems and I can't seem to make friends. I hate the house. I wish I had somewhere else to move to but I sold my house in Pennsylvania to come here."

"Let's see what I find," I suggested and headed out into the bright afternoon.

The house was set on a corner, the entrance on one street, the driveway to the garage on the other. Directly across from the front door another street rolled down the hill, the energy forming an arrow aimed at the front door considered in Feng Shui, cutting Chi, which diminishes beneficial energies.

That was only the beginning. As I walked each inch of the property I found the densest grid of Hartmann lines I'd ever encountered. Every single area of the house was affected by a line. My client's bed had two lines bisecting in the center. No wonder she was ill and getting worse!

Moreover, the lap pool she'd installed to help her back, "the reason I chose this design" was crisscrossed by four more lines. The stool she sat on at the kitchen counter, to take phone calls, was also on a Hartmann line. And because of floor to ceiling windows along the front of the house, the energy rolled in with no sense of support or privacy. Now I understood why she'd met me at the front door with, "Tell me right away if I should move. Two psychics have told me I should."

"Let's talk about what I'm finding," I suggested, interrupting my normal pattern of getting every bit of evidence before a conclusion. Quite honestly I wished she'd chosen some other Feng Shui practitioner. Suddenly I felt very tired.

"I had a friend over and we had a big argument right here in this room," she began. "And the contractor screamed at me." A feeling of fuzzy lack of focus washed over me.

"What are your options?" I asked.

"I'd like to move but I don't have anywhere to go right now and I'm too sick and I can't take a hotel with my little ones." She glanced down at her charming furry friends with affection.

"So it would make sense to you to do our best to improve the energy here whether you decide to move or not?"

She thought for a moment: "Yes it would."

"Let me take a closer look."

As I walked through the house I noticed more clues; a clock in the Health area had frozen at ten to seven; a cat recliner blocked the door to her Fortunate Blessings deck; in her Relationship area stood a pot of kitchen knives; the first thing you saw when you entered was a spiky plant; and in the Creativity area of Helpful People was an odd, star-shaped mirror that radiated out in small fragments of light.

It was the mirror that revealed the heart of the matter to me. What it represented to me was the child of wonderment wishing on a star, doing her best to create something magical. Somehow the usual cures didn't seem to fit. This house was different. The principles I usually used seemed hardly up to the challenge. She was telling me how everyone she'd met had ripped her off. I felt constricted inside. I wanted to go home. Then suddenly the feeling cleared and I knew the answers.

Slowly I began.

"Tell me what happened when you were five years old."

She described a childhood trauma that made me feel like weeping. I said gently to her. "And yet you managed to keep your sense of wonder and beauty alive. Look at that mirror." I pointed to the star.

"I bought that mirror when I decided to move here. It seemed so beautiful and magical and I was sure I'd have a wonderful time here."

"Yes. What we've forgotten is that this house is your baby. If you were to give birth to a handicapped child, what would you do?"

She was taken aback and silent. I watched her face soften. Then she said in a different voice, "I'd love the poor little baby." I felt tears in my eyes. We sat without saying a word. Then she said, almost in a whisper, "Oh, my poor house. Please forgive me, house. I'm so sorry for the way I've not appreciated you."

I outlined a recipe of steps to balance each area. Then together we put together a blessing ceremony and walked slowly room to room, the animals following solemnly.

Before I left she said, "This room feels brighter already. I see, the secret is to love the house. I've never really turned it into a home."

It was difficult to believe the change in her face. She actually seemed to radiate a different energy.

A week later she called to say, "I'm sleeping profoundly for the first time in two years and people are coming out of the woodwork to help me. I think we've started something." ꧁

Chapter Forty Two

The Power of Gratitude

*R*ecently, my friend Marie-France and I were remembering the Red Circle of Healing workshop in Taos, the one to help us develop our intuitive skills.

"When you told me I'd be doing what you do, I figured you'd got it all wrong," I told her. "But you were right. Feng Shui is all about intuition."

"Yes, and your work with childbirth all fits in too," she said. "After all, what is our first home? Our mother's womb!"

Looking back, every step of my journey makes perfect sense. I went from helping women give birth, to birthing myself, to helping others give birth to their full potential, using the principles of Feng Shui.

Feng Shui is a powerful tool to help us SEE, the first step in creating harmony in our lives. As you've read the cases in this book, you've explored the way in which outer clues reveal our inner lives.

If you'd like to play sleuth in your own home, I'd suggest you walk slowly from room to room, starting with the basement.

Are there doors blocked? Cluttered, congested areas? Piles of things you're not using? Things you'll probably never use? Chances are there's somebody out there who can use them. Clutter is the first obstacle to smoothly-flowing Chi.

Once you've completed your inspection, take a look at any artwork. Where did you get it? What does it represent to you? How do you feel about it? You may discover that a picture you once liked no longer holds any appeal.

Which room makes you feel happiest? Why? Is there an area you don't like? Why not? The moment you begin to ask questions, to apply these principles of awareness, your adventure is launched.

As you embark, take time to appreciate each change, no matter how small.

I fervently believe that it is important to acknowledge the many fortunate blessings in our lives. Every night before sleep I thank the Universe for nine of these blessings which happened that day. To keep Chi flowing we must constantly honor the gifts we create, the people who exchange service with us.

Each blockage we remove in our homes, each adjustment, helps create harmony, and since everything is connected the ripples are far-reaching. Ultimately, I believe harmony is created on this planet by first addressing individual harmony.

I wish to express my deepest gratitude to each person who has helped me on my Journey. I wish to thank my clients for sharing their lives. I wish you many Fortunate Blessings!